Adult Ballet

From Beginners to Intermediate

By: Seira Tanaya

Please see your health/ballet professional before using the information in this book.

www.adult-ballet.org

www.balletlove.co

ISBN-13: 978-1499554731

ISBN-10: 1499554737

© Adult-ballet.org 2014

"I always loved you, from the first time I saw you dance."

DEDICATION

This book is lovingly dedicated to you, my ballet teacher.
Thank you for all of this.

A NOTE FROM THE AUTHOR (and disclaimers)

Why did I write this book?

This book is a reflection of what it may be like pursuing ballet as an adult. It is my hope that you will find inspiration and ideas on how to start and progress in the journey of learning ballet as an adult.

In this book, I share my stories and discoveries about learning to dance ballet properly, despite the challenges of starting as an adult, such as finding the right teacher for my needs, locating a suitable studio and classes to suit my schedule, and other issues like the need to improve flexibility and coordination. There is also not much of a clear path for adults who wish to progress cleanly to advanced levels and dancing on pointe.

During my personal journey of learning ballet as an adult, I found it very hard to learn and progress properly, like most students do when they begin ballet as a child. Since I wasn't going to be a professional or bring fame, and I'm probably not even particularly talented, most top ballet teachers weren't interested in me. The few ballet teachers who agreed teach me, at times made me feel as though they didn't quite care if I was progressing, as if I was another cash cow.

There are many, many challenges in learning ballet. Ballet can be extremely difficult to master.

However, we adults face different challenges than a child. I do not think that it is necessarily harder for an adult to learn ballet; it is just different.

As I explain in the following chapters, we have different constraints and limitations but that should not stop anyone from perusing ballet.

Learning how to overcome each unique challenge as an adult ballet student is the key to progress. As an adult who has learned ballet mostly in my adult years, I made it a quest to discover how to overcome these challenges, to push the boundaries in my ambition in order to dance to the best of my ability.

Thus, through a fairly lengthy journey and relentless research to personally improve my dancing, I not only met many ballet angels who pointed me in the right direction, who showed me, taught me, and shared with me, I also managed to get myself into the world of proper ballet training, a world filled with solid pedagogues and professionals.

I now take classes with pre-professionals, which are quite different from the usual adult ballet dance classes, even if the adult ballet dancer has been dancing for years.

I am also pursuing a teaching certificate in ballet, which I took out of interest and passion.

I feel as though I've finally had access to the 'real stuff' not often taught, seen, or heard in adult ballet open classes.
This book is comprised of the information I've gained during this journey into the world of ballet as an adult. I've learned a lot from my teachers, professionals, adult dancers, semi/pre-professionals, and even children.

DISCLAIMER: I am by no means a ballet professional nor am I qualified to give professional advice on the great classical art of ballet. Please see your ballet teacher or healthcare professional before attempting to use the information in this book.

Chapter 1: Adult Ballet

I wish more adult ballet dancers would know this.

They, too, can achieve high standards.

I'm glad that the world is changing. The world is more accepting of dancing ballet as an adult, and many now realize that ballet isn't just for children.

The more I dance ballet, the less I think of ballet as an activity just for kids. How can it be only for kids when it is so tough, demanding, and difficult?

The kind of ballet that you see in children's classes in recreational studios? *That is not ballet.* At least, that is what I think in my heart.

Of course, it is ballet. It is just not the same ballet as we adults experience in adult open classes.

Children's ballet is still important. It lays the foundation for the REAL ballet they experience when they get a little older. Such classes are important because students learn the basic positions and postures, and they train their bodies to be flexible. Flexibility isn't something children have to struggle with like adult ballet dancers.

So, does it matter if you haven't learned ballet as a child?

No, you can still learn ballet as an adult. Sure, those who have learned ballet when they were younger will have several advantages to adult beginners. However, that doesn't mean you can't catch up with hard work. After all, the truth in the ballet world is that nobody is equal anyway.

We are all born with unique bodies; some of us have physical characteristics that make us more suitable to dance ballet. A suitable ballet body type will make dancing ballet easier, but that doesn't mean that the person with the less ideal body type will not be able to dance ballet!

Regardless of your previous experience with ballet, we all begin from different starting points anyway. It is what you do with what you have, and **KNOWING what to do each time** you face a roadblock or challenge that will make the difference in your progress in dancing ballet. You will progress faster and more efficiently if you face each challenge head on.

For ballet, *secret* knowledge is power. Why do I call it a "secret"? I call it that because certain knowledge just isn't as accessible. Teachers from all over the world may repeat it, but each student interprets it differently. The quicker your mind and body understands secret knowledge, the better. However, as you will soon discover, this is no simple task.

And it's also true that some teachers are just better at dispensing these ballet truths than others.

Some of this knowledge comes from pre-professionals and professionals while other knowledge comes from physiotherapists and other healthcare professionals. If you're not in the same 'world' as them, it is hard to gain access to this information. And even if you obtain their knowledge, they often speak a language that is so foreign it would take a long time before you truly understand what they were communicating.

As someone who has always been something of a researcher, I truly enjoy researching a subject matter to the ends of the Earth. I enjoy interviewing, observing, reading, and experiencing all the ins-and-outs of my subject of interest...all its secrets, tips, and tricks.

I've probably read every ballet book available, watched every video, and talked to as many professionals as I could find. I've done thousands of classes: private, group, Vaganova, RAD, and all sorts of classes that were available to me. I've spent hours and hours stretching, foam rolling, using *TRE*, ultrasound, and so on.

The most incredible thing I experienced in learning ballet was the moment when I started to believe that I *could possibly dance like a ballet dancer*.

Everyone has different aspirations when dancing ballet. Any one moving to music in a ballet class could be *dancing ballet*. Some just want to be able to turn a pirouette or do a grand jeté. Others might want to dance in the advanced classes someday. As for me, dancing like a trained professional was the epitome of my ballet aspirations.

Like many of you, my journey to becoming an adult ballet dancer began as a childhood activity and a dream, but it remained in the hands of adults. That is, until I became an adult. Being an adult is powerful. As adults, we are more in control of our lives, especially of our time and money. We have the ability to make decisions and take action.

I am genuinely excited about my ballet discoveries and am passionate about sharing them with all who are interested.

I hope that this book will serve as an inspiration to help you believe that you, too, can attain your dancing aspirations.

Chapter 2: My Ballet Story

I danced ballet as a child, from about 5 to probably around age 8 or 9, or maybe even less. I stopped dancing ballet because there was a time when I had no one to take me to ballet class.

I remember clearly missing ballet at age 10 but thinking that I was *too old* to dance ballet. (I remember having that thought on the large stony steps of Upper Bukit Timah, standing outside of my piano teacher's house, with grass as tall as me on each side.)

Yes, I think my story is rather common.

I also remember that year after year, many of my friends slowly disappeared. They also stopped dancing ballet.

I do wonder if they came back to ballet as an adult like I did. Even if they did, I probably wouldn't have recognized them.

I always dreamed about dancing ballet, and dancing was my first love. I remember dancing in the hallways of my flat. My most favorite outfit to dance in was a white nightgown with ruffles at the bottom. I loved the way the nightgown moved around my ankles as I danced in my lyrical fashion.

The way I was raised in Singapore conditioned me to think that dancing was not as important as other pursuits, such as getting into leadership programs, project awards, science projects, speech contests, inter-school sports competitions, all of which I did and excelled at.

My parents weren't the most sophisticated kind and being a rather peaceful bookworm, I graciously accepted the halt in ballet classes without protest or fight. They were adamant that I did well in school and my dad made sure I knew that the science faculty was the most important of all and made sure that I got into the Pure Science stream.

I wrongly believed that, at age 10, it was already TOO LATE for me to learn ballet. Looking back, there was no way I could have known that it wasn't too late. I didn't speak up about how I wanted to continue dancing ballet, since I thought it was too late.

At that time, Singapore was still undeveloped in the arts. We only had one program for teaching ballet to children and it was run by the Royal Academy of Dance. Girls were placed in grades according to their age. Since I stopped ballet for a few years, I was far too much of a beginner to be placed in Grade 4, which was probably where all the 10-year-old girls went. Thus, I let my dreams of learning ballet slip out of my little fingers.

I then took up ballet again at age 18. How? This is how it happened:

The trouble with pirouettes

During my university days in Australia, I took a lyrical jazz dance class and I couldn't do a *pirouette* – a turn performed balancing on one leg.

It was embarrassing doing the travelling steps that included turns. I was shocked and scared but bit my lip and tried, as I was determined to do it. I spun really hard and almost tumbled onto the ground. Michael Montgomery from the Sydney Dance Company was so gracious and came up to me and said, "Let me help you." I really enjoyed dancing lyrical jazz but I was I was so embarrassed by my performance.

In fact, I was a little too embarrassed to go back to class, so I looked through the papers for advertisements for ballet classes. Somehow, in the back of my mind, I knew that ballet was the foundation of dance and I figured out that learning ballet would help me in my lyrical jazz class.

I was determined to do the turn, which I later found out was correctly termed as a 'pirouette'. I made a promise to myself that the moment I mastered the turn, I would go back and try that lyrical jazz class again.

Well, hahahahaha.

At that time, a turn was just a turn to me. If I could get around and not feel like I'd fallen off my chair, then I'd done a turn. I had no clue about the intricacies and all the glorious details of a pirouette.

So who would teach me this pirouette? There were a couple of studios in my area, but I picked the one furthest from me. Noted dancer, Vanessa Lee Price, called it the VL Dance Academy.

There was a bus right outside of my apartment and its last stop was right in front of the studio. But that was not the reason why I chose this studio.

The reason I chose this studio was because I naively misread the ad. It read, "2 years to professional".

I thought, 'Wow! Just two years to become a professional?'

I thought that all I had to do was devote myself for two years to become professional. That was fantastic! I would graduate from university with my degree and also become a professional ballet dancer!

Of course, what the ad meant was that the studio offered classes for children as young as two years up to classes for professionals. But I didn't know that at the time.)
So, I called up the studio and went to meet my first real ballet teacher.

Obviously, it wasn't long before I realized it would take me longer than two years to become professional.
Thinking back on that fateful first meeting, I had no idea that it would give me a second chance at ballet. It was an early Sunday evening and I took the bus to check out the location of the studio. As I arrived, the sun was gloriously setting. The studio was locked, so I called the number on the door.

Vanessa picked up and I explained my situation, saying that I would like to learn ballet. She asked me if I wouldn't mind waiting for another 20 minutes or so and she would come to meet me.

What I didn't know at that time was that she was on her way back from the Blue Mountains, which was at least more than an hour away.

She had rushed back from her otherwise leisurely journey just to meet with me. She told me that she had started her dance studio not too long ago and that she was passionate about her students.

I told her that I had little experience in ballet, some experience in some hip-hop and jazz, and I was 18 years old. In the professional ballet world, being 18 years of age is generally believed to be too late to learn ballet (if you want to dance in a professional ballet company someday). She didn't have adult ballet classes then either.

Vanessa then offered to give me a trial class one morning, since most of her ballet classes and my college classes were in the afternoon.

I spent the entire 30 minutes of that trial class learning how to *plié* – which is, bending your knees in a certain way. I remember being shocked at how hard it was to *plié*, for something that looked like simply bending my knees. I was sweating buckets. I also remember feeling exhausted and was aching the next day.

I don't remember much else, but I knew that I wanted to come back. I even forgot that I initially only wanted to take private class with her to learn that *pirouette* so I could go back and dance lyrical jazz.

Before I left, she asked me if I wanted to buy a pair of second-hand ballet leather slippers for $5 AUD. What a steal! I agreed. First of all, I didn't know where to buy all the ballet gear, and I would have probably been too intimidated to do so.

I kept that first pair of ballet slippers for a long time due to the sentimental value.

After that first lesson, I went back home and checked my savings account.

It was a separate account from the money my mother had sent to me for school. I had about $2,000. It was money I had saved up since I was a child, from birthdays, Chinese New Year *Ang Paos* (red packets), and pocket money or small sums that I had earned doing little jobs. I thought I could use that money to invest in my ballet education.

Since I did not have much experience with ballet, and I was kind of old to join the seven-year-old classes, Ms. Vanessa and I discussed the best possible path for me to learn ballet as an 18- year-old student.

She was sensitive to my budget and asked me what I would want to do. I thought about my savings of $2,000 and my weekly pocket money. I figured I could do 2–3 private lessons a week, costing $40 each. She agreed and then threw in all the group classes for free, which she said I could attend when I'd made sufficient progress with her.

Shortly after my first trial class, she started teaching me the pre-elementary and elementary syllabus by the Royal Academy of Dance and prepared me for exams. I remember thinking how ridiculous it was that even my eyes had various positions in my dance.

The free enchainment part scared me and I decided not to take the exams. I also had enough exam stress from school.

I became really thin from ballet, and ballet changed the shape of my body. I ate double the amount of food and naturally found myself drawn to healthier food. I also noticed that, whereas I used to enjoy slouching on furniture I was suddenly aware that I preferred sitting up straight.

I also remembered aching all the time, eating every 2–3 hours, and becoming very slim and fit. Once my T-shirt shrunk in the wash and I only realized it after I put it on because a little bit of my mid-section was showing. I was late for class and decided to go to school without changing. Though I was slightly embarrassed, I had a toned body and I thought I didn't look too bad.

My ballet journey pretty much ended there. I became really busy in the final year of college and I ran out of funds. I also felt guilty using my mother's money. I later moved to another city and couldn't find a good and inspiring teacher. I took random open classes and my ballet dreams once again slipped out of my fingers...

Now, if this has happened to you, take heart! You can attain what you had again if you're willing to put in the work and be smart about it.

After many years of slouching, of having bad posture due to working at a desk and working on the computer, I grew overweight, had bad posture and backaches. I had a forward neck posture like a turtle, rounded shoulders and an anterior tilted pelvis. It made my stomach bigger than it really was, plus I looked pudgy and not toned.

I tried all sorts of things, spending lots of money on my hair, facials, make up, and clothes. I felt I was always trying to hide some parts of my body, or trying really hard to look and feel great. The point is that I was always trying to **hide**.

I decided it was time to do something. I did some yoga classes with friends, signed up for the gym, bought a Wii Fit, did brisk-walking, and so on. I did lose those extra pounds, but I just *wasn't feeling it*. Exercise felt like a chore.

I then remembered how the weight rolled off me when I was dancing ballet back at age 18. Inspired, I ordered $200 worth of ballet videos off of Amazon.com; white Sansha canvas ballet slippers that were on sale, and a portable barre for home use.

I started doing some exercises at home. Obviously, it didn't quite work. You can't teach yourself ballet, unless you're a professional!

Defeated by my own smart-ass idea to 'beat the system' and to train on my own, I looked for adult classes. It took a lot of courage for me to sign up because it was so intimidating. I actually registered twice on websites but didn't turn up for class. I was 29-years-old at that time.

Finally I did.

I dug out my old ballet slippers, wore a sports bra, grey racer back tank top, and black yoga leggings. It didn't occur to me to bring a water bottle.

First Adult Ballet Class

The first ballet class was intimidating. I still remember one of my friends, whom I still dance with today, walking in. She was the last person to enter the studio and had a sort-of ballet dancer gracefulness.

She stood in the middle of the class and was the most 'dressed for ballet class'. She wore her hair up in a neat bun with a pink scrunchie over it, pink leotard, and tights with a chiffon translucent pink skirt. (I guess she must have really loved pink.) She had the right posture and remembered all the steps and combinations. She had the ideal height of a female ballet dancer, about 5 feet 6, with a long neck, arms, and legs with narrow shoulders and hips.

I thought she looked like a ballerina. I thought she was one of those who could turn professional.

This story is important to me because I want to remember what it was like being a complete ballet beginner and the kind of 'beginner eyes' I saw ballet through. It is interesting to know that professionals and more advanced students see ballet with different eyes. Professionals have powerful eyes. They'll be able to see things and details that we cannot see. As a beginner, you'll see differently because your eyes are not yet accustomed to processing all the details of ballet.

I managed to get through the class, and thankfully, the class didn't have the travelling pirouette combinations. If it did, it might have scared me away.

That's why I really understand the fear some adult beginners experience; they either stand at the back of the class, refuse to try, or never come again. I hope that some of the information in this book can help to address these uncertainties.

At the end of the class, the instructor said to me, "Haven't taken class in a long time, huh?" I didn't know how to react to that statement, as I wasn't even sure whether it was a good or bad thing. Upon reflection, I have decided that it was a good thing because the instructor probably saw that I had prior training, no matter how little.

My friend, let's call her Hiro, seemed to get lots of attention and correction in class. She was popular and confident. She often stood in front and everyone in the ballet class relied on her to remember the steps. If she got it wrong, everyone got it wrong.

At that time, I didn't know that she took private lessons from the instructor himself. For a year. What a difference private lessons make!

Nevertheless, I continued with my group class and after each session I came away panting and my body ached for the following five days. During class, I remember my ankles were so weak that I couldn't *relevé* (tiptoe) very high. I couldn't stand on my tiptoe for long either. My heels barely lifted off the ground. When my best friend picked me up after class, he said to me that he has never seen my face that red before all his life!

After experiencing that one group class, I was hooked. I started taking adult ballet classes three times a week from then on. I secretly wanted to be one of the best in class.

In my mind, I wanted to be like Hiro, who was beautiful and elegant, and appeared to be conquering the steps, not struggling.

After taking classes three times a week for a month, I felt a little stronger and did not ache anymore. I still hadn't lost the weight I wanted to lose but I enjoyed the beautiful music and dancing. I remembered being really stiff and I was unable to touch my toes, lest put my tummy on my thigh.

In term of weight loss, I didn't lose weight immediately because, without real ballet knowledge, I wasn't using the right muscles. However, any movement for adults is still good exercise. So I did lose weight eventually, starting after my third month, but it was only after learning about ballet technique that my body truly changed.

Eventually, I became a familiar face in the adult beginner scene of that studio, and I started to make friends. I also formed a habit of talking to people who looked like they had classical training. I was eventually introduced to my first instructor, with whom I inquired about private classes.

My first private lesson

My first private lesson began with me learning to point my feet, as well as learning standing positions and *pliés*. That was it. I was sweating buckets and my body ached a lot after. It was depressing. My instructor was very strict and it seemed liked nothing I did was good enough.

At that time I was used to my Australian teacher, who was more encouraging. It was over time that I learned to read this negative feedback as a good thing. It was nothing personal. I learned to take every form of 'scolding', 'feedback', and 'correction' into my conscious awareness; and every correction I conquered meant that I was moving one step closer to looking like a classically trained dancer.

After trying a few different private and group lessons, I chose to study with two to three teachers who I felt were good for me in different ways.

I took a combination of open classes and syllabus classes. Open classes are those that have no set work and syllabus classes are classes that teach from a syllabus with pre-determined steps and learning objectives to meet. The syllabus classes were by the Royal Academy of Dance.

In the past during my university days, I was too afraid to take ballet exams, and now being older, I decided I wanted to do it. After a year and a half of intense ballet training, I sat for my first ballet examinations by the Royal Academy of Dance at the Intermediate level and passed.

I then submitted my application form for the ballet-teaching program and am now pursing the teaching route. Upon graduation, I will be awarded with a certificate to teach ballet studies.

Yet, all of my progress in ballet began with one simple goal: All I wanted was to find an activity that would make exercising something I enjoyed and looked forward. Simply put, that is why I went back to ballet.

In the very beginning, I had small ballet dreams. I wanted to be able to dance confidently and securely in a beginner's class. I also wanted better posture, and to be fit and toned.

I wanted to learn a dance variation (a dance number) and so I joined a syllabus-based class.

As my training progressed my goals grew larger and I realized that I wanted to look like a properly trained dancer. In that way, adult ballet did many things for me.

Many people asked me, "Why do you go to so many classes? Do you want to be a ballet teacher? Do you want to be a professional dancer?" (Of course, most of them didn't know that it is almost impossible for any adult to turn into a professional ballet dancer.)

To me, taking ballet regularly is like those who jog every day. No one asks joggers if they want to jog for a living or take part in marathons. It is just something that they choose to do. With little free time and resources, many of us feel that we need a reason to do things. That's the way adults think. I've learned to turn a deaf ear to that because doing ballet as an adult is not exactly the most rational thing, especially at the intensity that I am doing ballet. Yet, it is incredibly fulfilling on many levels, and for me that is enough of a reason to continue.

Chapter 3: The Adult Ballet Dancer

Anyone who is above the age of 18 and learning ballet for the first time is considered to be an adult ballet dancer. Actually, in the ballet world, anybody over the age of 15 is considered an adult ballet dancer. So, if you begin after the age of 15, you are placed in an adult ballet class because there is 'no place for you' in professional ballet training.

Why is someone over the age of 15 considered an adult ballet dancer? That is because it is probably too late for that student to turn professional.

It also depends on the studio. Some studios are very pre-professional student-focused, and others are more recreational. The pre-professional focused studios would probably put you in an adult beginners' class.

Also, if you are over 15 and you want to turn professional, I suggest you take private lessons right away, so you can still have a shot at turning professional. You have about three years to prepare for an audition. That, of course, depends on a lot of factors, which I will cover later in this book.

Who are adult ballet dancers?

There are a few types of people who make up the adult ballet dancer community.

Adult ballet dancers are generally those who:

1) Took ballet as a child.
2) Are professional dancers from other genres.
3) Took other dance forms as a child.
4) Did ballet but did not turn professional due to having the wrong body type or injury.
5) Have no prior dance experience but who have a strong interest in ballet or dance.
6) Are looking for a fitness activity.
7) Just love ballet for the music, posture, etc.

Of course, if you're one of those with no prior experience or someone who did not dance as a child, you might feel that you are lagging far behind. Let me tell you this in hopes that it will encourage you: Ballet has a way of escaping the body. As I've been watching my friends in class I can safely say this, those adult ballet dancers who started out with no prior experience can improve far beyond those who took ballet since they were children.

You can catch up. You can even get better at technique and dance ability than those who have had prior training, especially if they have not bothered to keep up.

There is, of course, no reason to be competitive, but the truth is that ballet is rather high maintenance. Now, this won't matter as much if your goal is to simply dance once a week and enjoy the social aspects of taking class with your friends and dancing to glorious music. Even when dancing only once a week, you probably will have the opportunity to enjoy classical ballet productions like Swan Lake and Giselle on a more sophisticated level. That's because your eyes will have become more familiar with the moves and your ears will recognize the music.

Adult Ballet Dancers

Think you're too old to start ballet? Here are some inspirational stories of adult ballet dancers.

Natalie Portman
You may already have heard of some famous people who started ballet as adults and achieved remarkable goals, such as Natalie Portman, who restarted ballet at 27 for her role in the film *Black Swan*.

Charin Yuthasastrkosol
Charin started her ballet training at age 47 and is a Guinness World Record Holder for Oldest Performing Ballerina. She still dances en pointe in her 70s!

Ella Hay

Another ballet dancer in her 70s is Ella Hay (75), who started learning ballet at the age of 37 at her daughter's ballet school. Since then, she has been dancing, teaching, and doing choreography.

Anne Hilary Sanderson

Ms. Sanderson started ballet at age 63! She is now 68 and, interestingly, she says retirement is a good time to start ballet. Although one is physically less pliable, it is an easier time to practice over "those with jobs or family duties [who] must find it more difficult to fit everything in". She also says she's having the time of her life!

David Wilson

David Wilson wrote one of my favorite articles about dancing ballet as an adult. Here are my favorite quotes from his article.

"One thing that people assume when I tell them that I dance is that I'm going to try to be a professional. I find this rather strange; playing tennis doesn't imply you're aiming for Wimbledon."

"Despite all that, I am still serious about becoming the best dancer I can be. I currently take, on average, three or four classes a week and rent out a studio at least twice a week to practice."

Adult Ballet Dancers Don't Dance Easy

On top of battling time commitments, a less physically active body, responsibilities, and everything else that comes with adulthood, adult ballet dancers may sometimes struggle with finding a suitable studio and a good teacher.

Not many ballet schools or good teachers take adult ballet students seriously in terms of offering them classical training (that they often need and want). That happened in my case, but I was fortunate to find a handful of teachers that invested in me, and because of them, I'm happy to be in the place I am now with my dancing.

Though you may experience some snobbery if you call a studio to enquire about adult classes, believe it or not, the ballet world needs us.

They need us to become adult ambassadors of ballet. They need us because we'll buy tickets and invite our friends to support the arts. We'll influence friends with our new ballet bodies and inspire them to take classes.

We'll buy tights and leotards and pointe shoes that support the businesses that fund the arts. And we'll send our daughters, sons, nieces, and nephews to ballet classes, creating more jobs for artists. We'll volunteer to help, we'll donate, and we'll raise funds!

The benefits for adult ballet students are far reaching, and most importantly, learning ballet helps adult learners appreciate ballet in a more sophisticated way. As adult students, we get to understand ballet and keep it alive!

Chapter 4: Motivations for Learning Ballet

Why do you want to learn ballet?

As the result of my blog, I have received many emails from adults who want to learn ballet.

Some of them ask me how to begin, or they ask me for extra tips. Many have no experience in ballet.

I usually send them a short friendly email or two and usually try to get a sense of what their motivations are for wanting to learn ballet as adults. For non-ballet people, it may seem like there aren't many logical reasons for learning ballet, other than to stay fit and enjoy the art.

Motivations for learning ballet

Why are your motivations important? Motivations are important because they will establish the types of goals and dreams you have and thus set the pace for your journey in learning ballet.

I will always say it is never too late to learn ballet.

However, if you begin as an adult it is probably too late to become a professional dancer in a classical ballet company. But hey, it is still not too late to become a professional, that is, if you want to become a professional. A professional means you can be a professional dance writer, a teacher, or become so good in your art that you are a professional ballet dancer, but with your age, no company will hire you due to the great supply of younger ballet dancers.

There are no incorrect motivations in learning ballet. Sure, there are some dance teachers who feel that certain motivations for learning ballet are silly, but I think it doesn't quite matter as long as it is your decision. After all, you're a full-grown adult, capable of making your own decisions.

If you are on the fence about beginning ballet as an adult, here are some motivations for learning ballet:

- Some are inspired by the beauty, grace, and elegance and want to achieve some of those attributes.
- Some are looking for a fitness activity.
- Some are looking for an after-work activity.
- Some just enjoy dressing up and doing a feminine 'sport'.
- Some want to refine their technique, and use ballet as a foundation for other dance arts.
- Some want to work on their posture.
- Some just enjoy dancing ballet to classical music.
- Some want to get better and dance in advanced classes.
- Some wants to wear ballet as a 'lifestyle badge'.
- Some want to train or retain their flexibility.
- Some want to keep the ballet technique they learned as a child.
- For others, ballet can be a social activity, something to do with their friends.
- Some want to be dance professionals, to become contemporary dancers.
- Some want to get on pointe.
- Some hope to dance a ballet variation eventually.

It might be too early for you, but I sometimes feel that you have to be clear in your goals for wanting to learn ballet. That way, it is easier for someone who has done ballet for a long time, or a teacher, to advise you on which path or what kinds of paths to take.

Of course, your idea for dancing ballet may change over time.

When I first started, all I wanted was to lose some weight. I did lose the weight, become stronger, and more flexible, and I looked younger too.

When I danced in my first ballet class, I was one of the worst. I was uncoordinated, couldn't quite remember or follow the steps. I was panting, I couldn't stand on tiptoe, and I was so inflexible. I admired the top few in class who looked confident and knew what they were doing.

Initially, I wanted to reach that level, to become confident in class and look like I had it altogether. I thought, 'I will be so happy if I can be one of the top few in the beginner's class'.

I even remembered feeling annoyed with those who looked like they just breezed through the class. Shouldn't they move up to the intermediate level and let real beginners like me have more of a chance to learn ballet?

It is only recently I've since realized why professionals or more advanced students still go back to beginners — to work on the basics.

My motivations, goals, and dreams have since changed since my first class. In fact, I became more obsessed with ballet with each class I took.

I wanted proper classical training and I was not satisfied being comfortable in a beginner's class. I wanted to be comfortable in intermediate and advanced open classes. I wanted to learn artistry and all the details. I wanted to look like a ballet dancer.

It doesn't matter if your motivations or goals for ballet change. It just helps to set the pace for your learning. If you would like to just dance and stay comfortable in a beginner's class, then once or twice a week of ballet class is good enough for you. With a reasonable amount of time and effort, as you would do for any other hobby, you'll be able to achieve this, possibly in about one year or so. Just don't give up or feel intimidated!

Ballet is also highly mental. The better you understand the ballet concepts given to you via instruction from the teacher, the more conscious you are of your body and movements, and the faster you can achieve your aspirations.

What if you are someone who realizes that it is too late to be a professional but want to pursue ballet with professional standards? Is it even possible?

I will now get this very commonly asked question, albeit a bit shyly, out of the way so it can set the expectations for this whole book.

The answer is yes. You can dance with professional standards. The price is high to pay, though, and what most adult ballet dancers and the general non-ballet population do not quite understand is that ballet is very grueling.

That is why professionals do ballet class every morning, for the rest of their dancing lives and some continue even after they retire.

The great news is that, yes, you can achieve a high professional standard, even in your adult age. There may be some limitations depending on how well you've kept your body free from injury and also your innate talent, but personally I've seen many adults who look properly and classically trained dancing in advanced open classes, right alongside the professionals.

If this is your dream, you have to understand that, first of all, unlike many other types of dances where one can turn professional in 1–3 years, the general time it takes to turn professional in ballet is 5–10 years of daily practice.

As you can probably guess, it requires a high commitment, resources, finances, and support, even though you're an adult.

The fees for ballet classes will add up and may be taxing on your pocketbook, especially if you dance daily. Ballet slippers and pointe shoes don't last very long, especially if you're using the right technique. Ballet is also quite time consuming, as there is also the issue of transportation and time. It will take time and effort to get to and from your studio, along with the time that it takes to do class.

Those evenings of walking your dog or having dinner with your family or friends will be a struggle, since most people work in the day and dance in the evenings.

And then, there are those extremely useful private lessons with the right teacher — those are as costly as professional ballet school fees.

The truth of the matter is that there are not many adults who can afford that kind of time and commitment, least of all to finance it all. This is for those who want to dance at a high level and reach professional standards. It is possible, but there is a high price to pay.

Nevertheless, I don't think these constraints should keep people from learning ballet. With a schedule of once or twice a week classes, many adults can still enjoy dancing and learning ballet.

I've seen both kinds of situations. There are those who start out passionately then kind of drop out of the radar due to changes in circumstances. There are also those who start out once a week and go on to dance daily.

Of course, there is nothing to feel embarrassed about in both situations! Not many people outside of your ballet circle will understand your drive to take classes anyway.

Chapter 5: Why it is Better to Learn Ballet as an Adult

If you feel too old to learn ballet, let me tell you why you are not. Learning ballet as an adult can be better than learning ballet as a child. Surprised? Read on. I've heard it all. Many adults tell me they've regretted quitting their ballet classes when they were younger or that they'd wish they had taken ballet as a child.

I am, in fact, one of them. I started when I was about five years old and stopped after a few years. I picked it up again in my teens and then stopped because of university and work. However, since getting back into ballet and meeting many professionals in the world of ballet, I can give you some reasons why it is better to learn ballet as an adult (than to start as a child).

So, if you're an adult who thinks you're too old to start, or that it's too late, perhaps after reading this chapter, you'll realize why it is actually a great time to start and enjoy ballet!

1. You are injury free

I think this is one of the best reasons to start ballet as an adult.

If you're like most adults in the workforce, most likely you're in decent or good shape, meaning you haven't worn out your knees, have tendonitis, torn hamstrings, or complicated ankle, knee, or back problems.

Okay, maybe problems with pain in the back are not unusual, but that can be fixed with good posture and a strong core that comes from learning ballet.

Many dancers who have started ballet since they were three find themselves coping with pain and injuries before they even turn professional! I've met some of these girls, some of them as young as 13 and 14 who have tendonitis. Torn hamstrings are common, as well as backaches. If you watch YouTube videos by aspiring ballet professionals, you'll find young 16-year-olds who are using ultrasound devices and painkillers to cope with pain...so that they can continue to take class.

Why? It is a variety of reasons. It could be due to poor training, turning out from the knees instead of the hips, muscle imbalance, and also due to the natural wear and tear of the body. The sad thing is that despite all that effort, only a few dancers are able to become professional. It doesn't seem worth it, does it?

My physiotherapist, whom I visit regularly to keep my body in the best condition as I possibly can, works with many professionals and pre-professionals and is a regular physiotherapist at my country's top ballet school. My goodness, I can't believe the stories she tells me about the kinds of injuries these young dancers (13–18 years old) have to cope with in order to dance. Some of these stories are pretty scary.

For instance, two friends who started ballet from age 5 had to pretty much give up ballet at 17 because of injuries. And I'm not even talking giving up professional dreams, but rather having to stop dancing altogether. It is difficult for them to take even a beginner's ballet class due to injury.

They both love ballet passionately, but now they can only enjoy watching ballet. One became a ballet piano accompanist. She wanted to teach ballet to young children, but it became very difficult when she couldn't kneel. The other one takes a class once every couple of weeks, and sometimes she has to forgo those classes because of sore knees. She is pretty much stuck in a beginner's class (even though she was in the advanced classes before her injury).

Even the professionals are not injury free. Every professional that I know is coping with some sort of injury or pain. My favorite two ballet teachers (who are ex-dancers: one is a principal and the other is a soloist) are continuing the rest of their lives with severe injuries. One is unable to kneel and the other has a bad back and waist.

As for us adult ballet dancers, we've been kept in good shape compared to all these dancers, who may appear to have an edge over us, but in reality, they envy us. We can dance as much as we like and our dance life is longer. I think that works because most of us really enjoy our jobs or families and we won't give them up to become professional (not that it is possible, but yes, in an alternate reality).

We can take our time to learn ballet and still be amazed by how much we can progress!

2. You are mobile

Being an adult, we don't have to rely on anyone to take us to ballet class. We are free to choose where and when to take class, how often to take class, and with whom to study. When you were a child or a teenager who hadn't learned to drive yet, you were often limited by your parents' commitments and schedules. Even if you did learn to drive, there is often the issue of whether you had a vehicle that was available. The kind of classes you took and with whom you studied were also limited to where you lived and how many viable options you had.

As an adult, all these issues are pretty much eliminated, or perhaps we can say we're in greater control.

I was made aware of this privilege because the minute I became mobile, I literally ran to take class in all sort of studios to find the one that was right for me.

3. You are financially empowered

As adults, the greatest envy children and young teenagers have of us is that we have money. We have the ability to earn it and are pretty much in control of how to spend our hard earned cash. When I was younger, I felt really bad having my mother pay for my lessons, especially when she was a single mother and I wasn't the only child in the family.

Back then, leotards and tights and shoes cost quite a lot more than what they cost now. I survived on three leotards (one bought on sale), two pairs of tights, and secondhand shoes for two years of ballet classes.

Now that you're an adult, you're in greater capacity to afford ballet lessons with no guilt.

When you pay for your own lessons, you might find yourself more motivated to learn and make it worthwhile compared to a privileged young person who might take classes for granted and see them as a chore.

Heck, you may even take private lessons and make up for all the time that you lost not learning ballet as a child. I'll tell you right now that it doesn't mean that people who took ballet as a child necessarily have more advantages than you. Sure, they will pick it up again faster, but even so, when they come back, they have to start again from ground zero, just like everyone else. Ballet has a way of escaping the body if it is not constantly trained. That is why professionals continue to take class every day for the rest of their careers.

4. You learn faster

Yes, you read it right.

I am always surprised to hear from very capable ballet teachers who tell me quite often how they enjoy teaching dedicated adults (much more than teaching young children), even though they know they're not going to go 'anywhere'.

Dedicated adults want to be there and have sacrificed their time, money, and have made an effort to take class consistently. Teachers are touched by their focus, hard work, and devotion. They also tell me that adults grasp ballet concepts much faster; for some, immediately or in a couple of weeks, which would normally take years for a young child to learn.

I take private lessons whenever I can afford it and I'm often flattered by my teacher's look of amazement when, within one explanation, I can correct an issue immediately and give her what she wants. She'll then explain to me how difficult it was to get her third graders (8–10 year olds) to understand.

The adult brain is more mature and capable of conceptualizing or using imagery to comprehend. It is more likely that the body control needs to be refined, which takes time, rather than because you didn't understand what the teacher was getting at.

I had a nagging suspicion that they're only saying that to be encouraging to me, the adult ballet dancer...until I had a chance to teach my six-year-old niece, who has been dancing since the age of three. To get her to turn out from her hip and to hold her arms using her back (inside of shoulders) has been a rather frustrating period. And I was only getting her to do those things to pose for ballet photos!

It is true. Your brain is more capable of learning ballet (and much faster) than most young children.

5. You might have a longer dance life

You're injury-free, financially capable, mobile, and in control of your life, and now you have picked up ballet with a passion. Ballet is your thing to do in the evenings and on the weekends. As a result, you've found a good teacher, made some ballet friends, and thus ballet is integrated into your life and you intend to keep it that way for a long time, if not for the rest of your life.

You might end up dancing far longer than you would if you started dancing as a child.

I've met so many people in the studio who have been dancing as adult ballet dancers for more than ten years.

On the other hand, I've met so many people who had danced pretty much their entire childhood, quit dance due to losing interest in dance (temporarily and with regret later) the minute boys became interesting, or who were overwhelmed by university and work, who grew overweight and could never get past the mentality of how thin they used to be when they danced (and as a result, a flat refusal to step into a dance class).

Some simply delayed getting back to dancing for a year, which became five or ten years, and they never had the courage to come back. Some, unfortunately, had injuries. Some became so discouraged from not being able to get a job in a dance company that they pretty much quit ballet. Some got so fed-up with the poor pay that they quit dance to pursue jobs that made bigger bucks. Many got married and became too busy with family and kids.

That is why those mothers who still dance in spite of having kids are to be revered and respected!

I have a friend who dances four times a week and has completed her RAD advanced exams at age 46. She is a mother of three. She stopped ballet at the first Advanced level to give birth to her first child, and subsequently continued to dance but not train for any exams until the other two kids were born, which was more than 10 years later.

I think that as an adult, when you chose to dance, something happens in your heart and mind. Dancing has become a love, a passion, a way of life, so much so that you don't think you're giving up something else to dance, unlike all these young people who are trained to think of 'giving up something of themselves' to dance. For us, it is a privilege. We're more aware of that fact because we're getting older and we realize that learning ballet is a long and hard road. It is no longer about priorities, but a chosen way of life for us adult ballet dancers.

There is also room for adult ballet dancers in the ballet world! There are many opportunities for adults to pursue ballet as a career aside from professional ballet companies.

What about the advantages of learning ballet as a young child rather than as an adult?

Sure, there are many advantages to beginning young. Obviously, young students have a chance to become professional and dance in a company. This also depends on a host of other things not within their control, such as if they develop the preferred body type, maintain good training, and take careful care of their bodies, as well as random opportunities, luck, and so on.

If you had started learning ballet as a child, these are some advantages:

- You'll probably be more flexible and this will be extremely useful if you have continued to maintain it.

- Because of all those years of learning ballet, your foundation in learning ballet will be stronger and you'll probably be in more advanced classes doing far more interesting things. You might already have developed artistry and are able to link steps better.
- You'll get to learn snippets of classical ballets and most probably, you have had plenty of opportunities to perform.
- You'll be able to mold your body, feet, and turn out to a larger degree to suit classical ballet.
- You'll have a head start in learning the other types of dances that adults perform, such as Latin, Ballroom, and Salsa. You'll probably have very nice lines.

But you know, since most aspiring hardworking ballet students don't turn professional anyway due to the wrong body type, injuries, and lack of opportunities, let's just say you don't have to turn professional to enjoy and dance ballet, so why not appreciate that you can also have a long dance life as an adult ballet dancer!

If you're careful, you won't wear out your body faster than the general population by dancing. In fact, you will probably be fitter and stronger than many others, not to mention, you will look younger too!

You can still achieve quite a large amount of flexibility; just look at all the grandma yogis (mature ladies who practice yoga). Many of them started yoga at a late age...late forties to sixties. Please read the chapter about flexibility as well.

If you meet the right teacher, or studio, you will probably have a chance to learn snippets of classical ballets and participate in their year-end performances as well.

So, for these reasons, learning ballet as an adult can be even better than learning ballet when you're a child.

Chapter 6: Your First Ballet Class

This chapter is for those who have no experience in ballet and would like to prepare to take their first class.

Have you always wanted to attend a ballet class but you are feeling really nervous? Fret not! Here is all you need to know about what to expect, how to prepare for it, and most importantly, how to pick the right beginner ballet class for you.

I'm always surprised to see a total ballet newbie (not quite the same as a ballet beginner) in my classes, whether I choose to dance at the beginner or intermediate level.

You can spot an absolute ballet beginner right away. They are either shoeless or wearing socks. Or they came well prepared wearing a pair of ballet slippers, either borrowed or bought from a ballet shop.

Sometimes they wear jeans or shorts with a T-shirt or a tank top.

The most telltale sign is letting their hair down.

I don't think they realize how hair gets in the way when doing little jumps or a forward bend!

While I don't mind having them in my class, they often are, unknowingly, more disruptive and distracting to the rest of us students.

I also feel sorry for the ballet teacher because these ballet newbies slow their class down. Some take pity on these students and try to quickly teach them basic ballet positions for their arms and feet.

Worst of all, many of these absolute ballet beginners get so intimidated and discouraged that they don't come back. That's quite sad.

That's why I think there's a disconnect in the meaning of a ballet class for beginners.

Maybe some of you can identify with what I mean?

Choosing a ballet class

It's a worldwide problem that beginner ballet class is not quite so beginner actually.

First of all, whenever you are searching for an adult ballet school, keep in mind that in most places, a beginner ballet class is not quite 'beginner' as most people understand it to be. You are expected to have already attended ballet class before, to know basic positions, and to have done barre and center work.

If you don't understand what barre and center work for ballet means, it means that beginner ballet class is not quite for you. (Unless, of course, there is no other option. If that's the case, then stick to it and try your best to pay attention and follow.)

Instead look out for 'Basics', 'Introductory', or 'Foundation' ballet classes.

As one website states, these introductory ballet classes are "predominantly designed for inspired adults with absolutely no prior training, and who wish to have trials or regular classes on ballet techniques."

The terms Basics Ballet Class, Introductory Ballet Class, or Ballet Foundation Class may be termed differently depending on the studio. In Singapore, Singapore Dance Theatre has an adult ballet class for absolute beginners called Basics. It has now been changed to 'Beginners' because of this problem. What used to be called beginner classes are now termed "Level 1".

At the Broadway Dance Center and Steps in New York City, they have beginner classes (for absolute beginners) and advanced beginners. Advanced beginners sounds like an oxymoron, doesn't it? It simply refers to those who have been dancing in beginners for a while and are familiar with the steps and structure. Yet, they may or may not be comfortable enough to attend an intermediate class.

If there are no such introductory ballet classes in your area, then what you could do is to watch some introductory ballet videos and read introductory ballet articles before joining an adult ballet class for beginners. It is also good ballet etiquette to call the school beforehand and let the ballet teacher know of your situation.

Basic arm and feet positions for ballet

Learn about the basic ballet positions for arms and feet on this webpage:

http://www.adult-ballet.org/ballet-positions.html

What you're supposed to learn in a basics ballet class

These classes are usually non-syllabus based but progressive.

- You'll be introduced to the five basic ballet positions of arms and feet.
- You'll learn proper body alignment.
- Simple but strong emphasis is placed on ballet foundation, such as basic barre work and center practice.

The class will also include *pliés, tendus, jetes, rond de jambe at terre* and *en'lair, fondus, releves*, and *grand battements*. These are ballet terminology. They are French; so do pay attention to how the teacher pronounces it. *Plié* are pronounced as PLEE-YAY and *tendus* are TONDOO

You may look up ballet terms online or download an app on your phone for it. You'll probably start off learning simple and straightforward combinations and these will foster body coordination, which is essential to dance.

It is normal to feel quite awkward in the beginning, but after a few lessons, these movements will feel more natural to you.

What to wear to your first ballet class

The Standard Ballet Outfit

The standard ballet outfit consists of a black classic camisole leotard and pink tights; pink ballet slippers with hair tied neatly in a bun. Generally, it is advisable not to wear any jewelry, with the exception of small stud earrings.

Of course, I wouldn't recommend you get into this outfit right away, especially if you feel a little bare in it now. This is, of course, unless the studio that you choose to dance in has a strict attire code.

This is what I'll recommend for your first ballet class.

1) Hair in a bun.

If your hair is too short, then tie it back in a small ponytail. This is unless your hair is in a pixie cut. Ensure you keep all hair away from your face.

To check if your hair is suitable for class, bend and touch your toes. If you have hair falling to the side of your cheeks, you must find a way to keep the hair off your face at all times.

2) Yoga/Pilates class attire

Black cotton cropped pants above the knees with a fitted fitness type top. This could be a fitted top, such as a tank top/racer back. And if you're female, wear a sports bra instead of a regular bra.

3) Ballet slippers (or socks).

You may wear these outfits until you have the courage to wear leotard and tights. Or you may choose to wear a leotard and cotton tights. Or you may choose to never wear a leotard and tights.

It is not mandatory to wear a leotard and tights as an adult ballet dancer, though it is advantageous, especially at the learning stage. I will elaborate on this in a separate chapter.

Anyway, most professionals I know get so sick of the standard ballet leotard and tights that they don't wear the tights when they turn professional. They still wear leotards, though preferring the fashionable types.

After a while, you can develop your own style for ballet class. However, just be careful that you don't go overboard and irritate the teacher. There is nothing wrong if you choose to be funky or stylish, but remember that ballet is a classical and visual art, which means most teachers are esthetically influenced and sometimes internally disapprove of what you're wearing!

For more details about how to choose the right dancewear for maximum improvement in dancing ballet, please read the following chapter.

"Should I buy ballet slippers?"

I have lent out my spare pair of ballet slippers more times than I can count. If you have a friend who takes ballet regularly, you might want to ask if you can borrow their slippers. Otherwise, wearing a pair of socks will suffice. (Better yet, call the ballet school to ask. Some ballet schools are strict.)

If you think you'll be willing to try ballet out for at least one term, or at least 5–10 classes, you could buy a pair. After all, you can get a non-designer one to start with, and they will cost about the price of two movie tickets or even less.

If eventually you decide ballet is not for you, you can always wear them as house slippers.

So You Had Your First Ballet Class

Regardless of how awkward your first ballet class may be, remember that you have achieved something!

Why?

You've wanted to do it and now you've done it. It does take courage to try something you've never done before, especially in ballet, which may be quite intimidating to some.

If you choose to graduate from your basic ballet class and take a beginners or advanced beginners class, the class structure would most likely be the same, as class would start at the barre, followed by center work.

The difference between these classes is that the combinations might be more complex and performed to faster music.

There will also be a pirouette section, which means turns balanced on one leg. Sometimes you'll turn on the spot, but most of the time it will be a travelling pirouette, which requires you to start from the back corner of the studio and do steps that require travelling diagonally across the floor.

Also, more jumps are incorporated. The ballet term for jumps is *allegro*, and it means quick and lively, which is the same way it is used in music.

There will also be a range of small, medium, and big jumps. The small jumps are generally things like petit assemble, or changement, where in your jump your feet lifts off the ground a few inches. Usually these jumps are performed on the spot. The medium jumps require you to travel a bit, to the left or right, forward or backwards. The big jumps require you to travel across the studio or from the left end to the right end of the studio.

These two sections of traveling turns and medium to large jumps may sound intimidating. I was so frightened the first time I had to dance across the floor with about 1 or 2 other people, with the rest of the class watching while waiting their turn. But remember that we're all there to learn. No one will laugh at you and the teacher will probably help you. It is important to have a thick skin and give it a try. If you don't feel confident just yet, you can tell the teacher before class and even ask for permission to stand behind and watch during that section.

Just don't give up!

Chapter 7: How Your Dancewear Affects Your Progress

I never quite knew how important this was until about a year after I began, when I realized how much difference AND progress I made due to what I wore in class.

Thinking of buying your first leotard?

If you've taken ballet for more than 6 months, or are absolutely sure that this is something you want to pursue for a long time, then perhaps it is time to invest in buying a leotard, if you haven't already.

If you can buy just one leotard, buy a leotard that fits the following requirements:

- It has a neckline that shows your collarbone or upper chest (camisole leotards, scoop neck leotards, tank leotards).

- It has a low back (at minimum; it has to dip until the bra line).

- It has to have the ballet-cut or high cut at the legs; and don't wear shorts with your leotard (as a beginner).

- It must be form fitting. It shouldn't sag at the bottom area; if it does, it is either too big or it's too old and it's time to throw it away.

Of course, it has to be comfortable. Bend, plié, touch your toes, kick your legs, do a port de bras sideways and see if the straps fall off, check your bottom to see if the leotard sags, or if it grabs too much.

The other additional features are that it should have extra support for your chest, if you're a woman. Leotards usually come with a bra-shelf lining or are double lined to give support and a smooth front.

When I first bought my leotard after coming back to ballet as an adult, I bought a few ill-fitted leotards. To be honest, I felt that I wasn't in tune with my body, thus I bought the wrong ones. I thought my leotards looked and felt okay. Looking back, my first few leotards either hugged my bottom too much or the straps dug into my shoulders. I also bought a couple ones that were too low in the front, resulting in me having to wear an additional sports/dance bra under them. That just resulted in me having to spend more money and wash more. Plus, it was more cumbersome.

After dancing for a couple of months, I grew more aware and sensitive to my body, the way it moved, and how I felt dancing when I was comfortable. Thus, my leotard shopping became more selective.

So why wear figure hugging leotards?

First of all, the leotard allows your teacher to see your form easily. She can correct your s-shaped back, or your protruding ribs.

She can see if your hips are not level with each other.

With a camisole or tank or short-sleeved leotard, she can see (more easily than she would be able to if you were wearing a T-shirt) whether your shoulders are level with each other, if you're raising your shoulders, or if they are hunched forward.

With a leotard that exposes your upper back, she can see if your upper back muscles are engaged, and whether you're holding your arms from the back or just using your arms themselves (the former is correct).

It is easier to see if you're pulling up correctly and not sinking backwards by arching your back.

Your ballet-cut or high-cut leotard will allow your teacher to see if the legs are turned out correctly from the hip and not the knees. Also, she can see if your inner muscles are engaged and whether your thighs are 'flat' when you're holding your leg in a passé position.

With a fitted ballet leotard, she can see from your back and the way you hold your bottom in, whether you're standing in the correct ballet posture with a straight plumb line or sticking your bottom out. She can see if you're pelvis is held straight and not tilted. Your hips are supposed to be facing up or frontal, not at an angle towards the floor.

If you do not yet understand completely what I'm saying, don't worry, just know that your choice of leotard enables your teacher to correct you more efficiently, thus you'll be getting the most out of your class.

My story: How my choice of leotard affected my progress

When I started ballet, I went to class in a racer back top with a sports bra, black-cropped stretchy pants, and a pair of leather ballet slippers. I did that for about three months before buying my first leotard.

Unknowingly, I conclude that I did the right thing, as my top was fairly fitting, allowing my ballet teacher to yell at me across the room, "stomach in!" That was one of the first major corrections that plagued me for a long time, and it took me about 1.5 years to correct. This was due to my flexibility issues, a weak core, and a general beginner's process of learning the correct ballet stance and ballet posture.

As I began to learn the right ballet techniques, I began to lose weight, and become both fitter and stronger, which led me to have courage to buy my first leotard.

It was a black camisole cotton-lycra Bloch leotard that cost $50 AUD, and I bought it on a visit to my brother in Melbourne. Now I realize that I could get many other leotards more inexpensively, such as www.balletlove.co (an affiliated online shop with free international shipping to www.adult-ballet.org).

The leotard has since been worn out. It has little fabric balls, it has faded, the slips have been adjusted twice and they are still loose, and most of all, it has started to smell. Nevertheless, I remember it fondly.

I remember trying on leotards in the fitting room of dance stores and feeling annoyed at how fat I looked. I didn't like how the cheeks of my bottom were squeezing out. I was also irritated by how the straps tugged at my shoulders. Finally, I settled for the Bloch leotard.

Ballet skirts are not recommended

Other than purchasing my tights and a ballet shoe key chain at the store...I got excited about something else. A ballet skirt!

Oh, they were presented in an array of colors at the Bloch store and I was addicted! However, because they were expensive, I only bought one. It was a navy one and I wore it all the time with my black leotard.

My other adult ballet dancer friends also liked it so much a bunch of them bought the same one. It was a difficult operation, as it seemed only available in Australia or through online stores in the USA. But someone would travel there and soon we started to have these ballet skirts in black, white, pink, etc.

I continued to wear ballet skirts for another half a year, because I was conscious of letting my bottom and tummy show.

Later on, I switched to a ballet studio with one of the best classically trained teachers in the country. She danced for many years as a principal dancer and was moved on to coaching and training semi-professional students before opening her own studio.

At the studio, the students were all serious and nobody wore skirts. I therefore had to learn to ditch my pretty ballet skirts and brave the class in just leotards and tights. I was nervous at first, but oh, that decision changed my life!

Looking back, I wouldn't have gotten the corrections and know what I know today if I had continued to wear that ballet skirt. Sure it looked pretty, but your dancing won't progress to be prettier if the teacher can't see below your waist.

When I ditched my skirt in my other classes, my previous teachers began to give me new corrections (and harp on the familiar ones, too). I realized that there was so much that I had been doing wrong but wasn't told because my teachers couldn't see my form.

Without knowing your problems, you can't fix them, and that just hinders your rate of progress.

So, whenever I see young students in classes wearing T-shirts over their leotards, I feel like telling them to take them off. Students can train a whole year but the teacher cannot see exactly how they are standing if they're wearing a T-shirt.

These youths take RAD exams, and during the exam period, when they have to do extra training and wear the examination leotard, they'll start to panic because they'll suddenly have a host of problems to correct so close to the exam time! And you can't wear a T-shirt during RAD exams. In fact, your examination leotard will have to be precisely what I've recommended above.

"Camisole leotard, scoop front neckline, mid-to-low back, ballet-cut leg."

I still love ballet skirts and I'll admit that I have a big wardrobe of them. However, I now save them for open classes with my adult ballet dancer friends where ballet class is more like a social activity.

In many adult open classes, the teacher might not put in a lot of effort to correct you, especially if they're not yet familiar with you and because they don't know if you're going to come back. Teachers save energy by only investing in the serious students.

So sometimes I don't expect lots of corrections with unfamiliar teachers and I just take this chance to wear my skirts. Of course, I'm also losing out on my own corrections because I can't see myself clearly in the mirror. But sometimes you just want to look pretty!

Ballet tights: Pink is recommended

I know most adults prefer to wear black tights. It is more slimming and flattering.

However, with pink tights, your teacher can see how your muscles are working and whether the right ones are working. They also can see whether you are straightening or pulling up your knees.

I know this from personal experience. I once had a teacher who would slap my knees all the time and give me lots of flak because they were not straight and I was not pointing with maximum energy.

I changed strategies and wore black tights to class and he didn't give me flak at all because they looked okay, or he couldn't see. What a big difference! I giggled and felt awesome that I didn't get as much scolding during that class. However, I quickly realized my folly and vowed to only wear pink tights to serious classes.

Through my other teacher, who is also as technical, I'm now able to see other people's muscles through pink tights and if they're working correctly or not. I've realized that I'm unable to see through those who wear black tights.

Thus, black tights are for those who have trained for more than ten years!

If you decide that you don't want to wear a leotard, please read my recommendations below.

What if I don't ever want to wear a leotard?

What To Wear to Ballet Class (if leotards are not an option)

If you don't want to wear a leotard, wear a tight-fitting top, ideally a camisole top with built-in bra support. The back of the camisole should be fairly open, ideally low enough to just cover the bra line. This is to let your teacher correct you if you're not engaging your back muscles. In the front, the top part of your chest should be exposed, allowing your teacher to see if you're pulling up your chest correctly and not by arching your back.

Otherwise, wear a tight fitting camisole top with a suitable sports bra that does not cover your upper back.

For bottoms, I would recommend tight fitting cropped long yoga shorts, preferably with your knees showing.

Ideally, you should wear pink ballet tights with tight-fitting shorts. This enables your teacher to check your knees, turn out, and to see if the right muscles are engaged.

For ballet footwear, you can wear socks if you're an absolute beginner instead of buying a pair of ballet slippers.

If you decide to buy some ballet slippers, buy the canvas ones with a full sole. The canvas allows the teacher to check if you're not scrunching your toes, and that your weight is mainly on the first three toes during demi-pointe/releve. The full sole is designed so that it provides more resistance to your foot, enabling it to develop stronger more quickly than a split-sole. Of course, split sole canvas slippers are more aesthetically pleasing.

I know this sounds incredibly bare for anyone who is not used to wearing tight fitting clothes, but I'll just say this is the best you can do for yourself. Why not make the best out of the time, money, and effort that you have spent on a ballet class?

Simply put, if the teacher can't see how you're standing, you can mimic the moves but you're not quite learning them correctly.

Many adult ballet beginners mimic how professional and advanced ballet students dress (a concoction of all sorts of weird things) and it is not recommended in the beginning.

Why professionals dress the way they do in class...they usually have specific reasons unique to them. Some want to keep part of their body particularly warm due to an old injury. Others want to focus on a lazy left knee, etc.

Many adult ballet beginner books recommend a T-shirt over yoga pants. I suppose they understand that many adult ballet beginners simply want to learn as a hobby and to appreciate ballet, rather than advancing to the best of their ability.

In conclusion, if you're just checking ballet out and want to try to get the most out of your time, money, and effort, wear some flexible clothing that will allow you to bend and stretch, and as tight fitting as possible so that your ballet teacher will be able to see your waist, bottom (as you advance, you'll later realize why), your chest, and your upper back.

Chapter 8: How to Choose an Adult Ballet Class (And why I prefer the small studio)

Not sure which adult ballet class to take? Here is how to choose an adult ballet beginner class.

There are many places to learn ballet or take a ballet class. When you first start out, of course, it is good to give every possible class a try. There are many factors to consider when you start a class. For most beginners, schedule and location (and sometimes price) are probably the top priorities.

However, as you progress, factors like type of teaching, teacher personality, or studio flooring, type of class, opportunities to perform, and number of students in each class become more important. Ultimately, everyone decides based on their individual priorities.

There is no wrong or right way to choose the right ballet class for you because everyone has different priorities. I can only share with you how I typically choose my ballet classes.

Factors to consider when choosing a ballet class:
(These are in no particular order or priority. I will later share about my personal preference.)

#1 Schedule

As adults, we all have varied and busy lives. Our class has to fit into our schedule.

Thus, what you can do is set aside time for class; for instance, I can dance Monday, Thursday nights, and Saturday mornings. Knowing this, I then look for classes in my area that fit those times. If ballet becomes higher on your list of priorities, you may find yourself adjusting your schedule to fit the classes you want to take.

#2 Location

Though it is increasingly convenient for adult learners to take classes, I've noticed that people in my country often won't travel for more than 40 minutes for a class. I've traveled up to an hour for each class but I stopped if I think that a class is not worth my time. This was especially true for a one-hour class where the studio flooring and teaching were not that good. Plus, if I had taken this class, it would have taken three hours of my time: one hour for class + one hour there and one hour back. The teacher has to be really good for me to consider travelling that far.

3 Types of teaching

Teaching method differs. Some teachers focus on posture, some tend to focus on expression, some placement, and others position, muscles, musicality, and other technicalities of learning ballet. They are all important to becoming a good ballet dancer.

However, some aspects may be more important than others depending on what stage you are at in learning ballet. Other teaching styles include a more encouraging atmosphere, a fun environment, or a serious and strict style. You may blossom under one teacher or feel down and out with another. It really depends on your learning style.

Generally, teachers that give personal corrections are the best. That is, of course, unless the teacher is not that good or is sloppy.

4 Teacher

Some teachers are deemed so good that students follow them, even if they switch studios or schools, or even levels (beginners/intermediate/advanced).If that works for you, why not follow your favorite teacher? If you feel that you really enjoy the class and the progress you are making, that is a fortunate thing.

For some years I couldn't find a teacher that I really liked in terms of helping me progress. That was quite demoralizing and it was hard to stay motivated.

Thankfully I have found some great teachers along the way.

5 Studio flooring

Some studios are really slippery (though you can carry a small bottle of rosin for that), thus you have to be more careful otherwise you could get injured, which will adversely affect your progress. Some studios do not have sprung floors, which are harmful for the knees in the long run, especially if you do a lot of allegro (jumps).

For me, sprung floors are important, especially at the higher levels because there are more medium and big jumps and pointe work.

Other studios may not have sufficient space, and are either too small in size or too small because there are too many students. That can be frustrating.

6 Opportunities to perform

I've known some friends who dance at the big open studios but take one class per week at a small ballet school. This is so that they get to participate in the year-end concert. Eventually I did that too. Performing is something that is hard to describe unless you have done it before, but it is incredibly rewarding.

As adults, we rarely get opportunities to perform. One of the ways to get a chance to perform is through your ballet school/studio.

Plus, you'll get to dress up and wear costumes. Imagine all the photo taking possibilities! (I'm well aware that not all adult ballet dancers look forward to having their picture taken.)

7 Number of students in the class

In general, a class with fewer students is better because you'll get more attention, space, etc. However, sometimes it is worth taking a crowded class if the teacher is very good.

Why I prefer a small studio

When I first started, I went for lots of open classes. These are usually adult ballet classes. It is rare to see anyone younger than 16 and if there are some of those students, they are probably practicing learning combinations or doing extra conditioning for their bodies for an exam/performance, or their usual studio/ballet school is closed for the holidays.

These classes are good to perhaps introduce you to ballet, and to learn basic terms and steps. It may be a less intimidating environment because almost everyone is a beginner. It is also a less intimate situation where you can just walk in, pay for class, not build any relationship with anybody, and walk out if you don't like the class.

That 'invisibility' may make it less intimidating to get started to learn ballet.

After a while, as I progressed, I realized I could progress faster through a small studio (and private lessons).

Benefits of a small studio

You are more committed to learning ballet

You pay by term, not per class.

Though this is less flexible for a busy adult, it forces you to make a commitment to going to class, even when you're feeling lazy. This is crucial to your progress in learning ballet.

Progressing in class together + extra motivation

Also, because your classmates are term-payers as well, you'll see the same people in class again and again. You'll learn to build a good working relationship in terms of progressing together. Not to say that it isn't competitive, but most likely in a good way, especially when everyone is grown up and mature, and that can give extra motivation to work harder in class.

If you have progressed, but because of the new faces in class each week the teacher has to slow down and not teach new steps, you won't be able to progress either.

Your teacher is more likely to 'invest' in you

The teacher will probably take a more vested interest in you if he/she sees you twice a week or every week. She/he gets to know all your habits, limitations, strengths, and weaknesses. This is beneficial for you because the teacher is more adept to see and push your progress. If the teacher sees new faces every week, he/she will not 'invest' in their students since they're not sure how committed they are and it would be a waste of time and energy, thus they tend to only correct familiar faces (if you haven't noticed that already).

If an open studio is the only choice available to you, try to attend a class taught by the same teacher more regularly and ask ballet technique questions after class. When the teacher sees that you are committed, they will likely give you more personal corrections. (Of course, there are some lazy teachers who still don't work much individually and only focus on general corrections in class. Then, what you'll do is personalize those general corrections. Imagine that the teacher is talking to you.)

Opportunities to perform + learning repertoire

Ballet, after all, is a performing art, and if you're in a small studio, you'll most likely be roped in for the studio's year-end concert.

In this way, you'll get to learn repertoires, which are excerpts from Swan Lake, Coppelia, Sleeping Beauty, modified versions but you'll still gain a greater appreciation for these classic ballets. And the next time you watch Swan Lake performed by the Royal Ballet or Bolshoi, you'll gain such a familiarity with the steps and the music that you'll be able to enjoy it at a much greater and more sophisticated level.

You most probably won't get to do this in a large impersonal studio.

Ballet Friendships

While ballet class is not social hour, for many of us, it is in some sense. It is the highlight of our week, where we go and de-stress, enjoy, have fun, see friends! Relationships can be built among your ballet classmates. You have a common interest and share tips, ideas, and help each other in stretching or with a difficult step. You may all go together to watch the ballet as well.

This is still achievable in big open studios, especially if you notice the regulars (such as yourself) and eventually friendships can be formed.

The friends I've made in class have brought a lot of joy to me. There's always someone to smile to, giggle with, or even make a joke like grabbing the barre for dear life when we do double pirouettes at the barre (this is not encouraged, but sometimes I do it because I'm goofy).

Of course, it's best not to chat to your friends during class because it is not good ballet classroom etiquette and is considered disrespectful to the teacher. It is also not conducive to your learning.

Most friendships are solidified outside of class, and through my personal ballet friendships I've been able to enrich my life in the following ways:

- Always have someone to accompany me to the ballet
- Have received discounts on tickets to the ballet, especially because we go in groups
- Traded shoes, tights, leotards, given away leotards, received leotards, etc.
- Combined dancewear orders to get free shipping
- Physiotherapy contacts

- Dance class referrals
- Website referrals
- Dance teacher referrals
- Coffees/dinners where we talk endlessly about ballet
- Photography jobs where I get paid to pose as a dancer
- DVD/YouTube referrals (which ones to watch)
- Stretching partners (to sit on you when you need that extra stretch)
- Someone to take a photo of me posing in your ballet gear (for my eyes only! ha-ha)
- Analyze steps, or have someone to ask for help
- Reviews about ballet or anything related to ballet
- Have someone I could borrow from when I've forgotten to bring something to class
- And more!

Chapter 9: Learning Ballet Terms and Combinations

One of the first difficulties of learning ballet as an adult is remembering combinations.

If you're like most adult beginners in ballet, you've probably stumbled into an open 'ballet beginners' class and pretty much mimicked movements from the person standing in front of you.

You'll probably continue to do so until about perhaps the 8th lesson, when some of the ballet terms become more familiar to you. You will feel more comfortable in your movements and will more-or-less follow the class better once you familiarize yourself with the terms.

However, if you were 'unlucky' and the only spot left was at the end of the barre, you might not have anyone to follow.

No matter how hard you try, you can't seem to remember the steps. So what to do in this situation?

Memorizing steps quickly

As a beginner, this is one of the stages of learning and possibly, a period that you as an adult beginner will struggle with.

There are so many things to learn: new moves, ballet terms, controlling your body, pointing your feet, etc. Most teachers understand when we struggle with remembering the steps. Ballet teachers don't like it, of course, but they understand it.

To correct this issue you must first of all realize that you have to be patient with yourself. Meanwhile, here are some tips that you can try to cope with this stage of learning ballet.

- Learn your ballet terms quickly. Learn what each move is called.

- Make sure you stand behind someone who is dependable in remembering the steps.

- Don't look in the mirror! Looking in the mirror at yourself slows down the learning process. Look at it sometimes, but try to see your movements in your mind.

- If you're consistently struggling with remembering the steps, the class is probably too hard for you. You're better off going down to a slower class. It is not wasted, you will learn better once you establish solid technique instead of using all your energy to memorize the combinations.

- Instead of memorizing, "3 tendus front, one plié", try remembering them in sets of 4 or sets of 8. Notice the slight pattern change in each set.

- If you're good at looking at patterns, <u>try figuring out the patterns</u>. Soon, they'll be very familiar to you.

- Try <u>singing your combinations</u> while marking the steps. "One, two-and-three. Twoooo, three-and-four." or "One, and two, and three, and four..."

When the teacher is demonstrating the steps, don't stand and try to memorize them using your eyes. <u>Mark the steps along with the teacher</u>. *Marking* means you do the steps roughly with less energy than you would when actually dancing the combination. This is simply a way to familiarize yourself with the steps. If your left side is weaker, use your left side to start the combination. This is to train coordination for your weaker side. Unless you still have a problem mirroring accurately then mark alongside with your teacher.

When you're confident enough, try one day to stand at the end of the barre. The reality of not having anyone to follow will force your mind to really focus on learning the ballet combinations.

Why do adult ballet beginners find it difficult to remember the steps

Adult beginners are typically not too familiar with ballet terms, and that makes it a lot harder.

When the teacher demonstrates a combination, he or she usually names a string of steps. However, only one part of your brain is engaged, the visual-part, because your brain does not bring up images of what is being spoken but rather processing the teacher's movements.

Also, your body and its muscles do not have a vast collection of references and memory, so every move is quite new and awkward. That is why it is important to mark the steps along with your teacher. This builds up 'experience' for your muscles and it will gain familiarity over time, thus requiring less effort to remember the steps.

Learning ballet terms

If you learn the terms quickly, your brain becomes familiar with them and hence you will find it easier to memorize steps. That is because you're memorizing in subsets, and soon you will start to learn combinations as you would when you use mind-mapping skills.

How to learn ballet terms?

Remember the terms your teacher uses. Repeat them under your breath. The more you say them and the more you do the steps physically (i.e. marking), instead of just standing there watching the teacher demonstrate, the quicker both mind and body register the step.

If you're in a slower class, and if your teacher is open to asking questions, go ahead and ask in detail how the step is to be perfectly executed. Of course, first and foremost, attend more ballet classes! The attention you give to a ballet term, the faster you will remember it.

Become familiar with the moves

Similarly to learning ballet terms, your body will take a while to register the movements and get used to performing them in one way.

Think your body movements like a car travelling on a long road full of twists and bends.

In the beginning of the journey, the car is unfamiliar with the boundaries of the road. It may travel onto the dirt path on the left, the sand on the right, and probably run over some bushes. As the car learns where the boundaries are, it is easier to travel within the markings of 'road' and 'grass'. It's not supposed to travel on the grass but on the road. Over time, your body will learn to move in a more exact way and not run onto the grass. See what I mean?

A few things you will need to establish yourself and stay on the "road":

- A good teacher who gives you corrections (the more the better)
- Frequent ballet classes
- The ability to recognize what is correct

- The ability to process information quickly and make adjustments
- Lots of visualization — imagine yourself executing the step perfectly
- You may also visualize by watching professional dancers execute steps

Why do children/youths have an easier time with learning combinations?

It is not because they are younger and have a better brain than you.

In fact, many ballet teachers tell me they enjoy teaching adults because their minds are so quick to understand, in fact, much, much faster than their young students! If that adult beginner is also very body-aware, they can learn very quickly and can catch up with ballet students half their age.

The problem most adult ballet dancers have is that their body is slower to do what their minds tell them to do. It is not because your learning ability is reduced, but rather, we're more used to typing at the computer, loading the washing machine, driving, and cooking. All of these motion pathways have been established for much longer. Learning to dance ballet is to learn new motions, to make new pathways for your body to move.

We've also lost quite a bit of body awareness due to being less physically active (well, most of us anyway). We don't play as many sports or run around, or walk even.

But you know what? Children these days suffer the same problems too. David Howard, a master ballet teacher, teacher to the ballet stars say that children these days take a longer time to develop coordination in dancing ballet. That is because they spend more time in cars, rather than walking, running, or riding a bicycle!

As an adult ballet student, you're probably only absorbing very little technique, but this is the process that we adults use to learn ballet due to how adult ballet is taught. In other words, we don't really have the opportunity or luxury that kids have, which is learning very slowly and through lots of repetition before a new move is introduced.

For instance, what we learn in an open adult beginner class typically takes six months to two years in full-time ballet school for youths.

Thus, the muscles of the children are worked properly and given time to build up a certain engagement, thus leading them to performing cleaner, more precise movements as their years of training roll along.

As adults, we're often thrown together in about three levels: beginners, intermediate, and advanced, though it is common to see people with different abilities jump all over. Adult classes are not as numerous as children's classes (unless you live in New York City), and people of different levels turn up according to their schedule, determined to work their body.

However, some ballet studios realize the difficulties adult ballet beginners have with learning ballet, so now they offer what is called a 'basic ballet class' or 'an introduction to ballet' class, or a 'foundation class'. They will start from the very beginning and teach you the positions of the hands and feet.

My overall message is don't be too hard on yourself when first starting your ballet journey. Be patient, but don't rely on the person in front of you forever!

As for me, I have no trouble memorizing combinations in beginner classes, and sometimes get them wrong in intermediate class, but in advanced class, I'm still struggling!

Chapter 10: Challenges of Learning Ballet as an Adult

An adult learning ballet for the first time or re-learning it all over again, faces different challenges from a young child. Actually, 'challenges' aren't exactly the best word to describe it. It is simply a different experience.

In fact, ballet teachers I know as friends seem to generally prefer teaching adults. That is because, unlike children...

1)   Adults are motivated.
2)   They learn fast.
3)   They are more focused.
4)   They understand instruction.
5)   Teachers do not need to discipline their adult students.
6)   They progress quickly.

A similar analogy would be, for instance, trying to teach English to someone whose first language is Mandarin, and teaching English to someone whose first language is French.

For the person who speaks Mandarin, the alphabet, phonetics, and grammar structure would be completely foreign. It would be his or her first time seeing a, b, c, and so on. This is similar to what teaching ballet to a child is like.

However, teaching English to a person who speaks French would be a whole lot easier than the former. That's because he or she is familiar with the alphabet and many pronunciations, even though it is not exactly the same. They are also more comfortable with the similar Latin structure of grammar. This is what it is like for an adult to learn ballet.

It is important to comprehend the specific challenges adults face dancing ballet. Understanding these adult-specific challenges will help you to be more effective in your approach to your studies, saving perhaps our most precious commodity as adult learners: time.

Overcoming these unique-to-adult challenges will help you look more and more like a dancer. You will start to look as though you've trained all your life.

So why do people think they are too old to learn ballet and that children learn ballet better?

Adults and children can both learn quickly but in different ways. Ballet is challenging for children because they cannot yet focus for long periods of time or control themselves very well. Most of them probably also haven't developed a focused interest or passion for ballet. They do ballet without questioning why they are doing it.

Contrary to popular belief, ballet is not simply mimicking or following steps. Real ballet technique is also extremely internal and mental. This is hard for a child.

However, children are generally more coordinated due to the greater variety of movements their bodies make each day compared to the adult, as children are constantly playing, jumping, and dashing around. Granted, this is an advantage but to learn to control of the body and use inner muscles still requires mental engagement. That is why children's classes are very slow.

Under a good teacher, as the years roll along, up until they are 15–16 years old, youths slowly develop more sophisticated muscle control and coordination than most adults, even if they are not talented students.

Adults need to develop coordination

That being said, I've also met many 15 year olds who have trained from age three who still dance with loose legs (a bad habit of feet not pointed to the maximum) and who are still unable to control their body. This is a result of poor training. Sometimes it is due to the child's lack of interest. Although I must admit that these poor students are generally still more coordinated that the adult dancer.

So, one of the challenges for the adult dancer is to develop coordination. It can be one of the hardest things to improve and it comes slowly.

Coordination is not simply coordinating the arms and the legs, though there is already great difficulty in that for the adult dancer. Sometimes the legs have to be fast while the arms move slowly in a totally opposite direction. To look like a classically trained dancer, he or she must coordinate the neck, head, fingers, eyes, and upper body. And there must be breath in the movement.

I believe coordination comes in different stages. That is how adults get through beginner levels to intermediate. First, the arms are held to the side in almost every exercise at the barre. They don't move while the feet are moving. That way, you can concentrate on executing the correct foot movements. When you get comfortable, you start moving your arms with your legs, slowly adding on the head and upper shoulders, etc.

How to improve coordination?

There are many ways, one of which is that the more classes you take, the faster your coordination improves.

I also feel that there are some teachers who create classes with more natural coordination than others.

However, sometimes it is not easy to identify the strengths of each teacher/class when you're dancing at the beginning level. Over time, you'll become more familiar with this. Similarly, you can take certain classes for certain specialties. For example, I now take some classes to improve coordination, others for turns, jumps or pointe, or for honing my basics.

I've also noticed that people who develop coordination quickly are those who take classes from a variety of teachers. However, some traditional ballet teachers also frown upon this. Ultimately you make your own decisions. We are also born with varying amount of natural coordination, so it is not the same journey for everybody.

Finding a teacher that will train you like a professional

One of the biggest challenges for the adult dancer is to find a teacher who cares enough to train you intimately like a professional. This depends on the place or country where you live.

It is a sad fact, but most open adult classes do not have teachers that are able to teach correctly. These teachers are not to be blamed entirely. I know many of them try their best but are only able to give general corrections.

Yes, it is true that there are many not-so-good teachers teaching adult classes around, but the reason why it is hard to get good teaching in adult classes is due to circumstances rather than the teacher.

Firstly, the adult classes, especially the beginner ones, tend to be overcrowded. It is simply impossible for the teacher to correct every student in this type of setting. Thus, he or she gives very general corrections. The problem with that is the student who needs correction may not know that they need to apply it. Since it is a general correction, they may just assume that it's not directed at them.

Secondly, student attendance is not consistent. Since these are open classes and are rarely term-based, you will see all sorts of new faces all the time. There are a lot of transient dancers. They come to class for two weeks then disappear for two months. It is thus hard for the teacher to teach in a way and enable everyone to progress at a somewhat similar pace.

Due to these circumstances, it is more likely that the teacher would 'invest' his/her time in the regular students.

Thirdly, in a beginner's class, the abilities of the crowd vary widely. It is thus hard to progress as a class, especially with the transient crowd.

For this reason, I recommend finding a teacher that you can 'follow consistently'. It is akin to getting accepted as an apprentice under some legendary Kung-Fu master. You'll study and literally live with him, and overtime you will become as powerful as he is. (I'm sorry for the cheesy illustration but I can't think of anything else.)

Another method would be to choose a syllabus class. This means that you'll learn a set of exercises that are fixed to certain music. You may do these exercises over and over again for a year. This way you'll be able to focus your mind on the details of performing a technique, instead of constantly memorizing steps.

This type of class is usually limited to children's classes. You might have to dance with students half your age, or ask permission for the studio to allow you to do so.

Time and commitment

Though ballet is quite an expensive hobby, I feel that what is more costly is the amount of time and commitment you've got to put in to learn and dance ballet.

Of course, this varies for everyone. For some people, once a week is quite 'costly' and to others it is easy to do once or twice a week. Even if you choose to dance once a week, it may not be easy. Thus, though ballet is a hobby, you have to set a priority to set that time aside for learning. Otherwise, it is quite hard to progress.

I like to think of it this way. We don't think of brushing our teeth or showering as a waste of time. It is not an option. We have to shower and brush our teeth!

For many of the general population who are growing more overweight by the day, the attitude towards exercise can be similar to the time committed to ballet (or any other activity for that matter). We all have to exercise to be healthy, but somehow we feel that exercise is optional. We do it only when we have time.

Thus, if we change our priorities to our health and make exercise (ballet class) non-negotiable, we can set aside some time to take a class or two.

Of course, I know everyone's circumstances are different. Maybe you are one of those who really can't afford time or resources to take a class. Whatever it may be, I hope you can get creative and get some ideas on how to pursue ballet.

Unfortunately, there are no short cuts in ballet. You can progress at an accelerated rate using some of the methods written in this book, but you still have to put in the work and the hours.

I mean, because we're all adults, you will seldom find teachers being extremely displeased at your poor attendance at ballet class. This is unlike in the children's school where teachers have the right to be upset at the child or their family when the child is away from ballet class for too long. Sometimes the child has to retain for a year due to poor attendance and thus poor or no progress.

The thing about ballet is that it is very easy to regress. You can be able to do a double pirouette comfortably, but if you stop class for a couple of weeks, your confident doubles will become a wobbly one. It is not like when you learned in school 1 + 1 =2 and can still produce the same result ten years later.

Thus, you have to align your ballet goals and expectations for progress realistically along with the amount of time and commitment you can afford to make.

People used to think (and they still do) I'm crazy for attending almost daily classes. I also agree with them and think I'm a little crazy for doing so as an adult. And *for what?* I ask myself, *it's not like I'm going to be making any money or a career out of this*!

But I feel passion for the art. Just as there are some people who jog every morning or evening as a way to keep fit, de-stress, and feel good, I dance ballet.

And then I met this whole community who dance daily like me. Here are some of the comments I hear in the locker room.

"If I don't dance, I get grumpy."
"If I don't dance, I feel really weird."
"I just need to dance!"

And suddenly, it's not so weird anymore. I found my family.

Of course, there's no judgment if you choose not to dance every day or if you can't. I'm very sure at some point in my life I won't be able to dance as much as I do now. However, I've set some ballet goals and I've committed 3–4 years into them. So for now, this is my life. And I really treasure every moment of it.

That's what happens when you're an adult, you start to realize how time is precious and dancing ballet is not going to get any easier as you get older, so you might as well treasure what time you have now. I don't feel I will regret my investment.

Finances

The good thing about being an adult is that we're in charge of our own finances. We have the ability to earn money and spend it the way we want to.

I don't know what kind of financial commitments you have, but ballet may get very expensive.

Professional dancers who are out of a job or whose contracts have ended have it the hardest. They have to find money to attend classes on their own (daily) to maintain their body and technique while they search for another dance job.

And then for females it is costly to buy pointe shoes. Some female professionals require a new pair of pointe shoes every day or other day. Imagine spending $80 every day on pointe shoes?

For males, they wear out their canvas slippers easily also. It definitely does not cost as much as pointe shoes, but yes, they wear out every week.

It will take a while for adult ballet dancers to reach a level where they are spending a lot on pointe shoes, but other expenses for ballet could include school fees/classes, leotards and tights, slippers, pointe shoes, concert fees with costume costs, examination classes, participating in examinations, and private lessons and choreography.

The thing about ballet is almost like putting money into a sinking ship. I'm not saying that it necessarily is "losing money" but you have to be aware that you're probably not going to see your 'money back'. The fruits of your labor are slow and may not be noticeable until perhaps months or years down the road.

The hard truth, which you will see in ballet studios everywhere, is that unless you are extremely talented, only those who can afford to spend will generally progress faster. This is the same in the world of children's ballet. The little girl whose parents put in private coaching every day is most likely to get the part of Clara in their year-end's Nutcracker performance.

In the same way, with adult ballet, the person who puts in the most effort, time, money, and is mentally engaged to understand ballet technique will probably see faster and greater progress.

I've seen some fairly talented adult dancers with some not-so-talented adult dancers who put in different levels of time, effort, money, and mental effort.

Sometimes the talented ones don't get very far because they don't come for classes or make the effort to learn deeper, whether through private training or finding a good teacher to follow or via syllabus classes. In fact, the not-so-talented ones improve much better and look more classically trained because they put in more time and money for better teaching, and sought a deeper understanding of technique.

But I mean, I also understand that sometimes you don't have to train like a professional. You can just enjoy moving and dancing in class no matter what level your technique is at.

However, if you want to receive the kind of training people who trained since childhood have, the best way to go is to follow a good teacher who will invest in you, join a smaller class or a syllabus-based class, or take some private lessons (under a good teacher).

Strict teaching: Feeling like a child

As an adult, we are more used to giving instructions, commanding, directing, demanding...and sometimes, giving firm negative feedback, or 'scolding'.

The kind of place where you learn ballet is quite infantilizing. Good teachers are often strict, and they may give you a lot of constructive but negative feedback every lesson, so much so that you may end up feeling hopeless and discouraged.

I guess this also depends on the culture or country where you will be studying ballet.

When I studied ballet in Australia, the teacher was more encouraging and would often say, "good" or "better". Instead of saying, "Why is your foot out of line?", she'll say, "Keep those feet in front of you."

However, when I studied with a teacher trained from the Beijing Dance Academy, I got scolded almost every exercise with 10 corrections breathed down my ear. Every lesson, twice a week, for many months.

Both teachers were good, but I actually progressed better with the strict teacher.

I don't think necessarily one style is better than the rest, but whether or not the teacher is more positive and encouraging, the key to look out for when choosing a good teacher is strict teaching.

As adults, it is hard to get used to strict teaching and being instructed as a child. Some teachers don't like giggling or chatting, even if you're discussing the exercise.

It also helps a lot to develop a thick skin, especially when learning under very stern teaching.

Sometimes you might be singled out for your wrongdoing, or the teacher may yell at you across the room. Your mistake may be highlighted to everyone or worse yet, you may be asked to demonstrate 'what not to do'.

You have to take this in stride. First of all, know that it is not personal. Second of all, remember that you are learning and actually YOU ARE THE ONE benefiting from this because you are receiving personal correction. It is like a mini private class without the exorbitant cost. The teacher actually LIKES you, because he or she bothers to correct you.

Many adult dancers wrongly think that teachers don't like them or are picking on them. Sometimes they just run away and do not attend that class anymore. I know, because I used to take it personally and sometimes even felt like crying! But I've since grown out of that and now I appreciate it, ha-ha!

The perspective of being singled out for correction is so different in a pre-professional school, where all the talented students compete for corrections. They feel extremely happy when the teacher singles them out for feedback, which means they are worthy of correcting. They feel that the teacher senses their potential and wants to make them better. They also enjoy the attention.

This is what you should do. Develop a thick skin and if you're getting scolded or corrected for something, take the time to immediately do the steps and attempt the correction. That's because you have the attention of the teacher, and you have one more chance for valuable feedback on a certain element.

The challenge of the 'No Touch' policy

Unfortunately, in most adult classes, there's a no touch policy, even if the teacher is female. It seems that it is rare these days that a teacher will touch you in an adult class.

I think this policy exists because, in general, the adult population does not feel comfortable being touched by someone they do not know on a personal level. Certainly there are always complaints, lawsuits, etc. to consider as well.

Yet, the reality is, learning ballet requires the element of touch. Sometimes, a lot of it! It is hard to get adult ballet dancers to understand that. I know some passionate adult ballet dancers who refuse to step into a class of a really good teacher because he props, pokes, and lightly slaps your position and posture into place. These adult dancers tend to be on the weighty side, and I can't blame them for feeling self-conscious and embarrassed.

Why do instructors do that? Why is it necessary to prod and touch and poke and scratch?

I do get that all the time — both from my female and male instructors.

The teachers do that to increase consciousness of your body to a particular area. Learning ballet means refining your body control, so that you can produce exactly what you picture in your head. However, sometimes because of the disengagement of your muscles, the muscles fall to 'sleep'. You lose consciousness of that muscle and become disengaged from it.

One example is the invention of paved, flat pavements. We walk on flat, even concrete pavements. It is comfortable, we do not have to watch our step or think about it. As a result, our core is mostly disengaged from it. Feel the difference when you walk on sand, or up a hill that has no paved pathways. Automatically your core is engaged to prevent you from falling as you move carefully on unstable ground. That is the reason why we are now a generation of weak cores and thus living with back and neck aches.

Similarly, in ballet, we have grown up into a generation with the least coordination and motor control because we generally do not use every muscle in the body. In ballet, we have to engage and use pretty much every muscle in our body.

If possible, try to find a teacher that still uses the old-school method of touch during teaching. In my ballet studies, we call it a 'physical correction'. The teacher comes and physically manipulates the body to achieve the results in hope that your muscle memory retains it.

I sometime slap and pinch myself during class, to increase more consciousness and awareness in a certain area. For instance, I tend to dance with my ribs sticking out, and sometimes when I pirouette. So, somewhere before my turn, I would slap my ribs a bit, press, or poke myself to let 'my body remember'.

Patience for adults

One of the hardest challenges that an adult may face in learning ballet is having patience. A good friend of mine who runs a pole dancing studio told me they once incorporated a ballet class for their current students so that they can improve their 'lines' (*lines* is a term used by the dance world to refer to the aesthetics of the shapes a dancer makes with her body).

The class started out very enthusiastically, with everyone in perfect attendance. As the class progressed, however, one by one students began dropping out of the class. Why? That is because they cannot see or feel that they are making progress. They cannot feel the difference and do not see how their dancing has improved.

I can't blame them. In many activities that adults do in their adult life, progress is quick. We are also living in a society conditioned for fast results. "Photos in 1 hour!" "Lose weight within a week!" "Achieve your diploma in 1 month!"

In other dance forms, such as salsa and hip-hop, you can attain professional/teaching status in 1–3 years. In other physical activities, such as Yoga or Pilates, you can get certified in a matter of months.

Ballet is an extremely cultivated art form with a history going back hundreds of years.

It takes a professional 5-8 years of daily training to attain their skill level. Judging from that, we have to NOT scale back expectations of how much we can achieve, but rather use a different standard of measurement of achievement as adult dancers. We can't expect to dance like a professional just yet. We have to exercise a lot of patience with ourselves.

I remember training with my friend for six months in a private class just learning *pliés*, *tendus*, and basic *port-de-bras*. This means that we learned to literally bend our knees, point our foot, brush the floor forward, sideways and backwards, and movement of the arms. After six months, we were strictly not allowed to turn but to *relevé* only, which means standing on tiptoe from fourth position.

It was frustrating, especially when we were paying hundreds of dollars for private class. My friend and I were so discouraged and we felt that we'd never be able to dance. The road ahead seemed so long and hard. But you know, my body now appreciates the strict and slow training, which became the foundation for my growth as a dancer and helped me progress to intermediate and advanced classes.

It is not easy to have patience. That is why most adult ballet dancers do not achieve a professional standard, unlike Yoga teachers or Pilates teachers who may start learning their craft at a later age.

Then again, I'm only speaking for those adult dancers who want to be classically trained at a high level. If your own motivation is to move and appreciate the ballet in a finer way, then you don't need to worry about having patience. Just go to class and move and enjoy!

Flexibility

Another issue that adult ballet dancers have is the issue of flexibility. There is this perception that they will never be flexible enough because they are not in their youth. All I can say is that it is proven that most people can achieve a great degree of flexibility that will be sufficient for ballet.

You also don't have to be flexible to begin ballet. You'll get more flexible *because* you do ballet!

You can enjoy and dance ballet even though you are not flexible. When you achieve a certain level, you may find yourself not satisfied at your current level of flexibility and would be inspired to stretch every day.

It is true that if you're more flexible, you'll probably have an easier time with ballet. It is also true that if you're flexible but very weak, you'll end up being a wobbly dancer, so flexibility is not everything. Sometimes the inflexible dancer is stronger and more stable when dancing, despite inflexibility with low extensions and a poorly arched back. Just as the flexible dancer has to work on strength, the strong dancer has to work on flexibility.

(See my chapter on flexibility for more information.)

You can do it

The challenges of an adult ballet don't only consist of the aforementioned issues, but becoming aware of them the first step in your progress!

Ballet may seem like a long and hard road, but you don't have to deal with every issue all at once. It is a journey to be savored one moment at a time.

Chapter 11: Ballet Posture and the Pelvis

One of the most important foundations of ballet is learning to dance with a neutral pelvis, and I sincerely believe that this is one of the greatest challenges facing the adult ballet dancer.

With good coordination, you can progress to the advanced levels without really mastering your pelvis, however you'll most likely not advance technically and will not look like a trained dancer. It may be the difference between one or two turns and quick jumps.

First of all, since the invention of dining room chairs, study desks, computers, and cars, people living in urban environments have forever altered our posture, gait, and balance from the way we were originally designed to move.

Coming back to ballet poses, the biggest challenge is often learning how to stand and move gracefully. We need strength and flexibility and a sub- consciousness that is in tune with the right way to move.

As adults, you can mostly say we have lost touch with our bodies. We aren't aware of how we use our bodies and how we move. We only notice something if there is pain or if we feel stiff. That's because we usually have busy lifestyles.

You can often spot a dancer from the crowd by the way he or she moves, or a person who is very elegant not just in looks, but in his or her carriage. In the past, good posture used to signify that that person was from the upper crusts of society. Now, it doesn't matter, even people from privilege no longer have beautiful posture or carriage.

Undo bad posture habits; Stretch out hip flexors

How you stand in ballet class does not come from that few seconds where you try to straighten up. You bring postural habits to the studio based on how you stand in your everyday life: in the office, the supermarket, at home, and so forth.

At the studio, when you consciously straighten your posture, what you're doing is actually manipulating your body against your current postural habits, which is enforced by muscle memory.

It often happens that once you focus on the steps you in turn lose consciousness of your posture, and your body once again reverts back to your less-than-ideal habitual posture.

You may also have tight muscles. These tight muscles result from long periods of sitting or standing. Thus, it is very important to stretch your hamstrings and hip flexors, which get tight from prolonged sitting.

You may look to YouTube for videos on stretching out the hamstrings and hip flexors. I try to do my stretching exercises before and after class.

Learning the right ballet posture takes time

Learning correct ballet posture while standing at the barre is the first step in forming good overall posture. It took me so long to figure this out. I couldn't tell the difference between me, the adult dancer, and the younger students in class in the way we were standing.

It is incredible that after three years of dancing almost every day, even in intermediate to advanced classes, I STILL have an issue with posture. My pelvis is not in a neutral alignment and my buttocks stick out. When I kept my pelvis neutral, it takes so much energy from me that I can't seem to devote energy to executing the steps.

For a whole year my teacher nagged at me about this and it was only after constantly being corrected that I could finally stand properly at the barre. I then had to be very conscious of my pelvis as I left the barre to ensure I kept the same correct alignment in the center.

So take heart! I'm not sharing this to scare you but the point of this is to let you know how slow the process might be.

In fact, the other day I was watching a video on YouTube about a girl who graduated from a pre-professional program. When asked about her struggles and what she had overcome and achieved, she revealed how she had no natural turnout, thus was unable to keep her pelvis aligned in a neutral position. She admitted it took her years. It made me realize that I'm not alone in struggling with this. Even professionals struggle.

A neutral pelvis

Of course, not every adult ballet dancer is going to be like me. Some of my adult ballet dancer friends have not much of an issue with this at all!

It is more noticeable after not dancing for an extended period of time, say perhaps a couple of weeks to a month. This is unlike cycling or swimming. You may not have done that for years, but you are still able to cycle or swim the next time you do it.

My teacher once said that a dancer's posture is one of the first things to go when they don't take daily classes. That's true for me. I feel that I have to work harder to align my pelvis if I had stopped dancing for a few weeks. Some dancers come into the studio and stand sideways to their mirror, checking their pelvis alignment, ribs, chest, and neck.

What is the right ballet posture?

Achieving good ballet posture requires a number of things. First of all, you must learn the meaning of good ballet posture. If you have a chance, stand sideways to a mirror and observe your posture.

Check it against this image:
http://www.elegantwoman.org/image-files/elegant-posture-woman.jpg

In general, your chest should be lifted, as though you imagine a balloon being tied to your chest (exact position is where you would place your hand over your 'heart') and let it float up. Imagine that someone is placing their hand over the back of your neck to pull it higher. Place your pelvis in neutral alignment. If you don't know what that is, please Google "neutral alignment of the pelvis". Keep your ribs in.

You're not only supposed to stand at the barre in this position, but at all times. Yes, that includes dancing in the center in this position. When you're in this position, you feel as though you're 'lifting' most of your weight out of yourself, away from your feet. It's almost as though you're trying to float during every movement. There's an upward sense, sometimes as though you're trying to stretch yourself as tall as possible. That is why in baby ballet, ballet teachers say to the children, "Stand as tall as you can."

Self-assessments are very helpful, but always check with your ballet teacher! Ask her or him to assess your ballet posture.

It is hard to learn ballet posture in an adult class

Learning the right ballet posture is very important.

Unfortunately, adult ballet dancers don't even get a chance to recognize the right posture. Why? That's because most teachers in adult ballet classes DO NOT correct posture issues. Maybe it is because it is overwhelming when everyone's posture is wrong! It would take more than 20 minutes of the class just to correct everyone's posture.

Unfortunately, many teachers often only invest in one or two students who they feel are really passionate.

However, ballet posture is fundamental. It is extremely important. If your teacher corrects your ballet posture, it is a sign he or she is a good teacher (and a hardworking one).

I also know this: Many adult ballet dancers who do not understand ballet at a professional level have made complaints to the studio and the teachers when the teacher spends 'too much' time on the basics. They get bored and they just want to move and dance. These dancers probably see ballet as some activity like Zumba or salsa dancing classes, where the most important thing is to have fun. Of course, there's nothing wrong with that.

A studio has to make money by pleasing its customers, so many teachers and studio owners have personally told me that they have to keep classes at a more 'interesting' level where they have coordination-challenges, rather than the focus on technique. I myself have tried an adult open class and was amazed at the difficulty of the class compared to the general skill level. When they focus on technique, these dancers would walk out of the class or complain. Thus, I suppose I can't blame the teachers who don't teach correct ballet posture.

Thus, you have to take the responsibility to learn the right ballet posture. Either find a good teacher or train your eyes to be so sharp that you are more conscious of it. That is also why I recommend wearing proper ballet attire...eventually, if that's a struggle for you right now.

Re-evaluate how you move and establish new healthier patterns

Unfortunately, we have spent many years sinking into our shoes, dragging our weight and feet along. Just look out onto the street, I'm sure you can spot at least a couple of people who move as though there's a downward pull in their steps. They look as though they're feeling weight at their feet all the time. That's the opposite of how ballet dancers look on stage. They look so light and as though they are floating and flying.

The body remembers and it became a habit. Now, as you know, all habits are hard to undo, but not impossible.

We have also spent decades sinking into ourselves, thus, what is an hour and a half of ballet class, maybe a couple times a week going to do to help reverse that? While it sounds impossible, ballet class creates an increasing consciousness that, if you constantly remind yourself about, will help you improve your posture!

For many years before I went back to ballet, I sat at a desk for about 10 hours a day. One day as I was all dressed up in a beautiful dress, with my hair done , and I caught my own reflection sideways as I walked to the entrance of the restaurant. I was shocked!

My shoulders were rounded forward, my neck sticking out like a turtle, my walk was sloppy and had a waddle/jiggle effect, my tummy protruded. I never knew how much working at the computer affected my posture and my walk.

Spot the dancer: The ballet dancer's walk

I always admired ballerinas in ballet documentaries or movies watching how they moved. I remember the opening scene of one of my favorite ballet movies, Center Stage, where they filmed ballet dancers walking to work. There is a kind of majesty about them, a sense of royalty. It was very elegant, but not in an elegant woman's way, but in a way unique to ballet dancers.

Fast forward, after my journey back into ballet, one day I caught myself in a reflection as I was walking. My first thought was, 'who's that?' and about a second later, I realized that it was me!

Now, I'm not saying I walk exactly like a ballet dancer, but it was a lot closer than that memory of awful posture and walk. At least, that image of myself fooled my brain for a while. Though I made a conscious effort to get into the right posture, I never thought it would create new habits in my daily life. That's when I started to believe that 1.5 hours of ballet training can bring changes in my life.

While walking in New York, I could tell who were the young students of the Joffrey Ballet School, not because they had buns and were wearing tights but by the way they walked together after class. They walked completely upright, as though they all swallowed broomsticks.

So, if you have issues with your posture, don't give up. Keep reminding yourself and working on it, and one day, without knowing it, you will realize that your posture has changed.

Muscle tightness contributes to your posture

Besides bad posture habits, the other issue adult ballet dancers have is muscle tightness. Contrary to popular belief, muscle tightness does not just come from exercise but through being in a stationary position for extended periods of time. For instance, driving, sitting at a desk, or on the couch are all postures that are straining to your body, making your hamstrings or hip flexors tight. Not to mention the rounded forward shoulders and forward neck due to working at a desk or at non-ergonomic work stations.

Tight hamstrings, hip flexors, and a tight lower back pull your pelvis out of neutral alignment, resulting in an inflexible back and lower back pain. You also might have a weak core from sitting too much, hence your ribs might protrude because your back is more s-shaped curved. Your ribs get 'locked' and tight, making it hard to 'keep your ribs in'. In some classes, the teacher constantly reminds adult dancers to keep their stomach and ribs in.

With reminding from the teacher, you can control your body to 'tuck the pelvis' in and keep the 'ribs in' along with shoulders back and 'ears back' (to keep the neck in a straight alignment with the body). However, due to weak core muscles and muscle memory from straining postures, we are unable to maintain this position, especially when we lose consciousness of it as we try hard to remember the steps.

So, what are we to do?

Core strengthening

We have to strengthen our core. There are plenty of exercises for core training that you can do. We also have to assess our workstations and whatever we do, whether it is on the iPad, watching television, or eating dinner at a table, so that we are more aware of maintaining good posture. We have to make a more conscious effort to maintain our posture.

As for me, I try to do sit-ups and reverse sit-ups, and hold my body in a V-shape while I alternate my legs in a scissor fashion (to train the inner thigh muscle). I also take as many classes as I can. During class, I arrive early and stand at the barre directly opposite the mirror, so that when I turn my head to the side, I can see whether I'm sinking into my pelvis or I'm upright and lifted.

When I'm in the center dancing, I try to think of lifting my body out of my legs as much as I can.

However, that may not be enough. I'm just sharing and speaking out of my own experience. For some, there may be too much deep tension in your body. Even if you had a strong core, you would be wasting too much energy fighting your old habits or your strong resistant body due to the high tension held in bad body positions/postures.

You'll have to find a way to release any deep tension you may carry.

How I fixed my ballet posture

This is my story. Back to a year before I sat for my Intermediate exam, I was reminded and reprimanded by my teacher for a whole year about my anterior tilted pelvis. With my stronger core, I was able to hold on to it for a few seconds but it would let go the minute I started doing the exercises.

I wasn't quite able to fix it, no matter how hard I tried. It would go in and out, which means my posture would be correct at times but I wasn't able to maintain it throughout the exercises.

Through a physiotherapist, who used a myofascial release technique, and a lot of pain bearing on my part, she pressed out my lower back, quads and hip flexors in one session. I couldn't believe it when my teacher exclaimed the very next day in class "One whole year I nagged at you, and finally it is correct."

It then dawned upon me that it wasn't that I unaware or not trying hard enough to maintain a proper ballet posture, I was fighting the tension in my body that had to be released. I was so inspired from that episode, that I managed to release the tension in my upper back, my ribs, my neck, my shoulders, and even my hamstrings through the help of my physiotherapist and other methods.

That is the reason why dancers roll out on foam rollers, tennis or golf balls and other devices.

I'm not exactly qualified to discuss how to release the tension in your body in detail, but what I can do is point you to several options where you can do your own research.

1) See a physiotherapist that uses myofascial release techniques.

2) Practice yoga and deep breathing.

3) Stretching.

4) Roll out your muscles using a foam roller or other devices such as a roller, golf ball, tennis ball, etc.

5) Use sports massage.

6) Use deep tissue massage.

7) Engage in imagination techniques (see Eric Franklin's books).

8) Rolfing.

9) ACM.

Some of those techniques contributed to my ballet posture today, something that makes me sort of stand out among the adult ballet community. I get asked if I'm a professional. I'm really not! The real professionals would be able to tell right away. I'm just sharing from experience how the right posture will make you look more classically trained than the dancer without it.

Chapter 12: Flexibility for Adults

Sure, you can start ballet at any age, but if you want to progress in ballet as an adult, you have to face the problem of flexibility and tackle it head on. This is a chapter about how I became more flexible learning ballet as an adult, or rather, how I had to become more flexible in order to progress. Disclaimer: This is not meant to be professional advice; I'm only sharing my experiences. Please consult your health professional.

Ahhhh, the issue of flexibility when it comes to learning and dancing ballet is close to my heart. The reason why I'm writing right now is because I'm not going to class today, nor did I go to class yesterday. Why? Because I'm healing from a self-inflicted injury (incurred by my wonderful physiotherapist)...all for the sake of becoming more flexible.

Truth: You don't need to be flexible to learn ballet

It is true that you don't need to be extremely flexible to learn ballet as an adult. An average person's flexibility is sufficient. Doctors tell me that if you can bend and touch your toes, you are considered flexible. Your hamstrings are sufficiently flexible.

So if you don't think you're flexible, don't let it stop you from learning ballet. After all, you will become more flexible as you take more classes. You'll be surprised with yourself, as I was. That is why I think it is such a waste that people let their own perceived lack of flexibility prevent them from starting ballet.

One adult ballet dancer friend I know took a whole year to master her splits before taking her first ballet class. Imagine how much faster she could have progressed! Nevertheless, she's doing very well now and learning a solo variation from Esmeralda.

Ballet teachers also tell you not to worry about getting your leg high in Adagio (slow lyrical movements) or in grand battements (big high kicks) if you cannot maintain a good ballet posture (because you're not flexible enough, yet). That is true and very correct. You'll need to train your body to move strictly in purposed pathways, just like you are trained to drive on the roads within the markings, you cannot compromise your alignment in order to get a higher leg. Otherwise, you're not progressing and wasting your time.

However, that may give the impression that flexibility is not important or not necessary to work on. Well, I know this because I was once under that impression.

It is true that you needn't necessarily work on flexibility while learning ballet as an adult and it will come to you naturally. With that being said, there is a limit to the extent of flexibility you will achieve through lessons.

Eventually you may reach a point where your lack of flexibility starts to annoy you because it is another roadblock to progress. If you have reached that point, congratulations! You must have worked hard and far to get to this point. This brings me to my second point.

Harder truth: You need to be flexible in order to progress

If you're fortunate to be in class with some advanced dancers, you'll eventually realize why flexibility needs to be worked on and maintained constantly.

Dancing becomes easier, requires less energy, and you will not be fighting with yourself but focusing on controlling your movements and expression. It is easier for you to learn new moves and choreography, too. Of course, you'll look nicer and closer to a ballerina with beautiful reaches and bends.

A friend who was very dedicated to ballet was told by her ballet teacher that unless she worked on her flexibility, she could not progress further.

Though I wasn't very flexible, I had never bothered to focus my energies on working on it and would rather spend my efforts trying to perfect double pirouettes and get comfortable with a triple. Why? My reasoning was like this: I am an adult ballet dancer, I'm not going to be like those young girls who have their feet above their heads in *écarté* position, and my legs were already high enough for my ballet exams and syllabus work. However, in a Eureka! moment I finally understood why becoming more flexible really helped in my progress.

To make a long story short, I pulled my hamstring and the pulling pain wouldn't go away for months, making sitting in my right split no longer possible, even if they weren't the full ballet split.

I decided to bite the bullet and see my friend's extremely costly but good dance physiotherapist. She fixed my hamstring, but found out my torso was kinked to one side. She fixed that too, and then my upper back, shoulders, and neck.

As a result, I discovered why my teachers had always pulled my shoulders back and yelled at me to keep my ribs in.
My ribs were too tight in an 'open' way. I had to buy this small rubber ball and lie on it, placing my tight ribs over it, for weeks.
I was too tight, and through physiotherapy, I loosened up and managed to overcome my usual corrections.

I realized it wasn't because I wasn't listening or learning right, it was my own inflexibility that I was fighting.

Well here I am a much more flexible and stronger dancer!

Two general types of stretching for flexibility

There are two types of stretching that you can do to become more flexible.

The first one is static stretching, which means you sit in a stretched position and hold for 10–30 seconds.

The second one is dynamic stretching, which means you're stretching in a moving motion, like the high kicks in grand battements.

When you're taking ballet class, you're really doing lots of dynamic stretching, like *tendus* (which means stretch of the foot), and *rond de jambres*, where you stretch the areas of your turn out. In high kicks, you're stretching for splits and your forward and backward bends help stretch your hamstrings and your back.

I've had some ballet friends who don't actively stretch, but find their legs getting higher as time goes by. Of course, they had to take lots and lots of classes to get that way.

How to become more flexible as an adult

Possible ways you could explore increasing your flexibility include the following:

Learn some ballet stretches

You need to learn to stretch your body in a way that is the most beneficial to learning ballet. No point stretching in a way that does not help you in your dancing. As you know, ballet is very classical and there is not much room for modifications of technique.

Do your stretches every day

Every time I asked flexible adults how they achieved their splits, they told me they stretched every day for a year and they continued to stretch daily.

I couldn't imagine doing that every day and that is why I did not achieve my splits for a long time. In the end, I gave in and started stretching every single day.

I started stretching after each ballet class for 5-15 minutes, and then later bumped it up to stretching at home on a yoga mat. I have upgraded to an Airex mat.

I can now do my splits, though it is not a pretty looking one or comfortable kind. But I like to tell myself that at least I can sit in my splits. My left split is a lot better than my right. If I don't maintain it, I feel I get set back a few points. I'm not yet to the point when I can go down (cold) and feel nothing at all.

See a physiotherapist

Different physiotherapists may use different strategies to work with your body. I'd say see a couple of them and find out which ones work for you. There was a period of time when I saw two different people because of the different things they did for me.

My first physiotherapist used deep tissue massage or sports massage. This technique is really painful but it releases years of tightness and helps you increase your flexibility. In other words, you can literally pay someone to make you more flexible without doing any work. You'll just pay a hefty fee and have lots of pain to bear. It was like nothing I have ever felt before! And I used to think my pain tolerance was high. She also taught me the TRE method (Trauma Releasing Exercises) to release tightness in my muscles.

The other physiotherapist customized my stretches for me. She realized the reason I couldn't do a perfect ballet split on my right leg was due to quad tightness in my back leg (my left) and I also had very tight hip flexors. She gave me homework and I saw her every 2–4 weeks to check my progress. Eventually, I did master a perfect left split, with a bit more work to do on my right splits. (Now I can do both, though I have yet to be comfortable in the side splits.)

Get a foam roller, foot roller, tennis balls, golf balls, *bed of nails*, and step on smooth stones for the feet.

You'll need to roll out your calves, thighs, and quads. Sit on golf balls, roll around on tennis balls, and lie on a bed of nails to release neck and shoulder tension and step on stones to help your feet.

This is, in a nutshell, helping to release tension in your body so you can gain more flexibility.

You may also view some foam rolling techniques on YouTube.

I've also used a "bed of nails" to release tightness in my neck and upper back. It took me a while to get used to it, but I was amazed at how much tension it must have released for me because I fell asleep on it!

As for the golf balls, you usually sit on them to release tightness inside your glutes and you place the tennis balls around your hip area and roll around them.

Ballet flexibility DVDs

These DVDs range from 40 minutes to an hour long. I find them effective, but you must do them every day for months. That is quite hard to commit to. I think I made it in the first month and went back to stretching in class and rolling around with tools and visiting my physiotherapist every now and then.

Breathe

Tell your legs and back to relax and breathe deeply, especially when you're about to go into something like a split. If you're anticipating pain, your muscles will tense up and you will be fighting your own efforts. You have to tell yourself to relax and let your body sink into your stretches. Touch your muscles and mentally command them to relax. Touching them will bring greater body awareness.

Imagine

I learned these two techniques (breathe and imagine) from a book called Dance Imagery for Technique and Performance by Eric Franklin. In order to release more tension, you have to use your imagination. This will affect your body in powerful ways. When you're feeling pain from stretching, imagine yourself made of jelly. See your back as jelly and wobbly. Imagine what happens when a jelly woman needs to touch her toes. Feel the texture and see the color, press it and see it wobble in your mind.

Yoga & Pilates classes

This is effective, but for time-strapped adults, this might be a challenge! Yet, even if you can only afford the time and money for one class a week, it will make all the difference.

Stretch class

If you have them in your area, go for it!

<u>My flexibility story</u>

This is my flexibility story and perhaps a continuation of my journey to become more flexible. I will write about what helped me too.

My flexibility in the first three months of ballet

When I first re-started ballet, I was really inflexible due to the years of long hours working at a computer.

This happened to me because working at a desk creates tight hip flexors and a tight lower back. When I did a port de bras forward (bending to touch my toes), my upper body made a 90 degree angle with my legs. I mean, it was fine, the movement was correct, most teachers don't mind it as long as your knees remain stretched. But when I looked at myself in the mirror, it wasn't how I imagined I should look.

Of course, I didn't care about flexibility then, I just wanted to learn my ballet moves. As I did hundreds more port de bras forwards, my hamstrings became more flexible, but still, when I looked in the mirror, it was as though I could fit an entire basketball between my head and knees, my body still looked like it was at a 90 degree angle.

I just assumed I would get better, but I didn't, at least not at the rate I wanted to improve.

However, I found that I could do my right and left splits after about 3–4 months of classes (three times a week). That was amazing, because I hadn't done it in so long. However, my splits weren't ballet splits. For a true ballet split, your pelvis has to be square. Mine wasn't. But still, it was better than nothing, and my teacher would typically come and lift me up, square my hips, and let me sit in them to stretch.

This might be different for every body. Some people's bodies are harder or softer in different areas.

My flexibility 4–6 months

After about four months, my friend invited me along to her private stretch class. Group stretch classes weren't available in my area, except from yoga and Pilates, so a few of my friends took stretch classes in the form of private lessons. We shared half the costs of the studio and the teacher.

In my first lesson, I couldn't sit and reach to touch my toes. In ballet class, when I had one leg on the barre, I couldn't bend forward to put my head to my knee. My body barely moved, and only my head and neck were forward. My teacher pushed me gently from the back. I felt my knee popping up and had to fight the stretching pain (your pain tolerance will increase as you go along). By the end of the one-hour class, I could finally touch my toes. I remembered the teacher saying, "Somebody can touch her toes now."

By the third or fourth lesson, probably over a period of six weeks, I became more flexible than my friend. My friend was known to be quite 'hard'. My teacher said I was 'soft', meaning that he could press me down further into a deeper stretch, but would stop because I was yelling in pain. My friend, on the other hand, was hard, and he said if he put a bunch of bricks on her, she would still hold up.

Don't worry too much about whether you're 'hard' or 'soft'. It really doesn't matter because we've all got our own areas to work on. In my case, one teacher told me I was soft, but in the end, another teacher and my physiotherapists told me that I'm really 'tight' (hard). So either way, I've got my own obstacles to overcome, and as for yourself, you have to find the areas in your body that are currently obstacles.

By the sixth month, I was fairly flexible, or so I thought that I was sufficiently flexible. I felt it was time to do other things, like learn how to do a balance en tournant!

I stopped stretch classes with my friend and told her, "I hate to stretch, I want to focus on building strength." At that time, I had my mind set on getting back on pointe as soon as possible.

I couldn't do side splits, but I could do imperfect right and left splits. I could hold my leg in one hand with foot around my head on both sides. I thought to myself, 'What other flexibility do I need to dance ballet?' I didn't think I needed to be any more flexible than I was, so I left it.

How foolish I was.

My flexibility month 6 to month 18: A full year later

When I decided to take ballet exams, I had to find a new teacher; one that could register me for exams and who was willing to teach me and let me into her class (in my country, this is not the general practice and most good studios are very snobby about it). I am so grateful for my teacher, who did take me in. However, I had to take class with her advanced students who wanted to take the intermediate exams because it was a compulsory exam.

Firstly, being double their ages was humbling, but also my lack of flexibility aspirations quickly surfaced. My teacher reminded me all the time that I had to 'kiss my knees' and 'to stretch more'. She didn't let me off or grant me any leeway just because I was an adult. I'm actually grateful that she didn't make any excuses for me.

I pushed harder and, as a result, I'm much more flexible than I ever was, though I am still one of the most inflexible in class.

Flexibility in the legs

I hated the pain from stretching, but as you learn to dance, you'll realize a certain sort of pain and discomfort are part of the process.

Most websites tell you to stop if you feel pain in stretching. I believe they are bordering on being safe. All I can say is that it is hard to differentiate a stretching pain and a harmful pain in the beginning. Whatever you do, proceed with caution and see your health professional.

I wanted to rely on ballet class to improve the flexibility in my legs, but it was not happening quickly enough for my liking. So I had to learn to stretch and reverse stretch to get by. If you're careful and do not pull your hamstrings, this area may be slow, but it is possible to get there without too much costs. Just regularly stretching and sitting on golf balls and foam rolling will often suffice. It is also fun, sometimes, especially in an open adult class, when everyone else is having the same problems as you, and you're all just doing the exercises and chatting and complaining about the pain together.

Flexibility in your torso and back

These are my problems! They are common problems of flexibility that adults have when learning ballet.

I was much too 'tight' (read: inflexible), like I was set in stone, and I had to exert more strength and waste energy to 'pull my shoulders' back and 'hold my ribs in', which affected my breathing. I was fighting myself. I was fighting against my tight set-in-stone muscles, and my body compensated with other problems.

Of course, if you do ballet leisurely, you probably can dance with these issues and not let them affect you and your joy for dancing and learning ballet.

As for me, I wanted serious classical training, so these issues affected my learning because I was an adult, and years of computer work had taken its toll on my body.

I began 'fixing my body' to gain flexibility in my neck, shoulders, and torso area by lots of stretching, rolling with a foam roller, physiotherapy sessions, ballet classes, and a more conscious effort on posture. I also tried using imagery to signal my body to release those muscles, and used TRE, and today I still use all these things. Following these techniques improved my dancing by leaps and bounds. I fight my body less and less, especially in my shoulders, to keep them back and down and relaxed and keep my ribs in. Especially keeping my ribs in!

Now when I see other adult ballet dancers having the same problems as me, keeping their shoulders less rounded, and their ribs in, and not being able to do a pretty back bend without their ribs popping out, I think about my previous problems and wish I could tell them what I know; what a big difference flexibility makes!

For flexibility in the upper back, you'll need several sessions of deep tissue massage. This is to reverse your accumulated posture of rounded forward shoulders.

In ballet posture, we're supposed to stand tall and proud, and you can't do that if you're pretty much 'set in stone' from years of working at a desk as an adult. Beware: it is painful. There's not much else you can do to get the knots out and release the muscle tension that is often so deeply embedded.

This also applies to flexibility in the lower back as well. For me, I fight an s-shaped back because all my life I've been walking with my tummy out and my upper body 'sitting' on my lower back.

In ballet, I learned to 'lift' the weight off myself and not 'sit'. But I'm currently paying for the years of bad posture habits. The problem with having a stiff lower back is that I can't hold my turnout well, no matter how good my turnout is. I'm always fighting my inflexibility, which always naturally pulls my hips, making me stick my bottom out.

Yes, I may correct it when I'm standing at the barre, but the moment I'm dancing in the center , I may not have a strong enough body to hold the right position. Even if I did, I'm wasting energy. At the end of the day, if I manage to regain flexibility in my lower back, I'll have a much easier time dancing with the correct technique. Then I can move on to other fun things, like artistry and interpretation.

Flexibility in the arms

For years, I wondered why my arms look so ungraceful. I had to increase consciousness of my arms, and that came by touching, slapping, and pinching my arms in class. Watching myself on video also helped.

I later realized that my right arm looks especially stiff because it was my dominant and stronger arm, and thus, held lots of tension. I consciously used my thumbs to press out my muscles during little breaks, like sitting at the traffic lights.

Arch flexibility

Over the years, my ballet arches had gotten better, though I'm not gifted with a pretty arch. There are a few tools that you can use to stretch your arch, such as the ballet foot stretcher. But use them with caution! There are several theories out there and different people have reported different findings.

Also, see your physiotherapist (preferably one who works with ballet dancers).

Flexibility in your turnout

Flexibility in your turnout might be due to several things. I remembered my turnout being better when I was much younger, even though I thought I had bad turnout. In the end, after seeing my physiotherapists and through lots of pain, my turn out has improved. It may be due to tight hip flexors and quads and a host of other things I'm not medically fit to explain.

Chapter 13: How to Choose
a Good Ballet Teacher

A good teacher is very important when it comes to learning ballet. Learning ballet as an adult means that your learning time is rather short, because ballet gets harder by the decade.

Due to the physical demands of ballet, it is better to try and devote as much time as you can and get over the learning curve *as young as you can*. Yes, it doesn't matter what age bracket you are in, you simply work from where you're at. Don't put it off. Naturally, we ALL wished we had started ballet earlier or continued when we were younger. There's no use regretting our choices, and no *more* time to waste.

Thus, finding the right teacher saves you a lot of time. You can progress more efficiently and not lose motivation due to your lack of progress.

I suppose progress can be hard to quantify, but when a student has made progress, it is quite evident in class. Even the adult beginners will notice it. Progress is usually made due firstly to a good teacher, secondly, to a good student. My point is that good teaching comes first, because as dancers, we cannot really see ourselves and correct our own movements most of the time.

It might take some time to find a good teacher. That said, there might be a few good teachers in your area, and if you have the luxury, you should learn from all of them.

As long as you feel there is learning, there is value. However, if you can't afford to take class from every fantastic teacher you meet, you can choose the one that you feel helps you progress the most.

So how do you know who is a good teacher and who is not?

One of the hardest things for beginners is figuring out who is a good teacher. There are some ways to determine good teachers, but not every method is foolproof.

Here are some ways to determine if your teacher is good:

1) Personal corrections

Personal corrections are a luxury. If you get some, you know that the teacher is hardworking or likes you.

There are some teachers who are not so hardworking. This means they don't really look carefully at students to correct them. They might give general corrections, such as, "turn out, knees to the side, ribs in." Students may or may not know whether the corrections apply to them at all.

2) Demanding teachers

Hardworking teachers will carefully show you how to do a step and explain the details. He or she will also walk around the room and try to give personal corrections to all their students.

Hardworking teachers are also demanding teachers. They will not be satisfied with you pointing 80% of your foot. My teacher often grabs my ankle suddenly to check if I'm fully pointing.

She is almost never satisfied with the alignment of my pelvis.

Another teacher is never satisfied with my shoulders or my neck, or that I'm not pulled up enough.

In a way, it takes a lot of effort from them to keep harping on the same thing and 'be on your case'. I feel embarrassed that I still do get corrected, but I'm grateful that they haven't given up on me.

It's true that some teachers think that certain students can't change, no matter the amount of feedback, and literally 'give up' on them, i.e. they don't bother correcting the student anymore.

I certainly do not want my teachers to give up on me! Thus, a good teacher is someone who hasn't given up on you.

Demanding teachers are also the types that are never satisfied with mediocre presentation. They want movements to be clean, precise, and correct. They won't let you relax unless you are at your very best. They will not stop correcting, reminding, nagging, etc.

You need that correcting because it takes a long time for good habits to form in such a way that you do not have to think about it anymore.

I've experienced both sides of the spectrum. I used to highly adore a particular teacher because he was always pushing me to do doubles and teaching me complicated steps. He wasn't a demanding teacher at all. He was satisfied with my butt sticking out, my ribs out, my rounded shoulders, forward neck, funny fingers, and non-fluid movements.

I took lots of private lessons from him. Later on, when I became better, I reflected and realize he had a double standard. It wasn't that he wasn't a demanding teacher; it's that he had one standard for me, the adult ballet dancer, and another for his pre-professional students.

He was satisfied with my imprecisions, as I, being an adult ballet dancer, would never be as good classically as his pre-professional students anyway. At least that's what he saw, so he just wanted me to enjoy dancing ballet, even though my movements are not so graceful or correct. Plus, he enjoyed the tons of money made through the private lessons of his adult ballet dancers.

I suppose I can understand his point of view.

Some adults don't mind that because they enjoy moving, even though they know they do not look like a classically trained dancer. They just want to keep up with the advanced class and get a work out.

I, on the other hand, have always had a different goal. I want to look like a ballet dancer, or at least like a properly trained dancer. So in the end, I felt like I wasted a ton of money. Nevertheless, I am still grateful for all those lessons, which helped me improve my coordination.

On the other end of the spectrum was a highly annoying teacher who frustrated me to bits. He was extremely demanding, crazy, insane, ridiculous, and he drove me up the wall each class. It was impossible to do what he demanded of me. I hated his class but somehow deep down I knew its value and had to always mentally prepare to be strong.

Eventually I did progress, by a lot, such that I would get comments from open teachers who had seen me in class. Students would come up to me and ask how I progressed so quickly. Students under his crazy teaching also progressed nicely and some are now dancing at the advanced levels.

Indeed, I have danced under a few teachers and the emotions I feel are still similar to when I first began. I still feel highly irritated and frustrated when I am critiqued. I feel as though my teacher is picking on me or does not like me.

However, due to my growing awareness, I've also come to realize that what I see with my eyes and understand in my brain is not in line with what the teacher is noticing, and I need to remember that when receiving a critique.

Sometimes the teacher is unable to communicate in a way that you understand, and that's to no fault of the teacher because we're all so different and there's not much time to explain in class when other students are also demanding the teacher's attention.

So, when I'm corrected now, I try my very best to figure out what exactly I'm doing wrong and try to align myself with what the teacher is trying to say, rather than taking it personally.

3) Physical feedback

The best kind of teachers will give physical feedback. They might tap you, poke, scratch, or slap you lightly (unless they have known you for a long time, then it might be a big slap). They might move your arm, body, hold your hips, grab your ankle, etc.

As an adult, initially that was quite shocking and it was an intrusion to my personal space. I have since realized the importance of it. There are some people out there who feel that physical feedback might not be appropriate and feel that they can learn as effectively with verbal feedback.

In my opinion, I feel that both verbal and physical feedback is equally important. You both need to engage the brain and the body. Using your brain to engage your body is useful but sometimes it is slow. Thus, a slap on your ribs will send stronger and many more signals to the brain to keep them in.

For that very reason, I sometimes slap and pinch myself. For instance, I will slap my hips just before I start a travelling pirouette combination. I want my focus to be on my hips because for me, thinking about my hips turning helps me turn better. When I feel the touch of the hips or the arms, my brain can 'zoom in' on them and the consciousness of how I'm moving or using them increases.

There are studies that prove that touch is a powerful tool for learning. Touch and feel increase the brain's connections with the physical body and the mind.

In tribal Africa, busy mothers cannot afford to spend a lot of time caring for a newborn, as they have to work hard to gather food, clean, etc. Thus, they always massage, touch, and do a gentle scratching motion to their newborns' legs. They bathe their babies in warm water and rub herbs around the legs. As a result, these babies start walking by 8-10 months. That is incredible!

In India, malnourished babies still grow fat and healthy due to an Indian baby massage that Indian mothers customarily do for their newborns.

4) Quality verbal feedback

Now, a good teacher will also give you quality verbal feedback. Not all verbal feedback is equal. For instance, a good teacher will tell you the intricacies of a step. Maybe not always, because there's always so much to do in a ballet class, but he or she might help you draw a connection. For example, we do *this* at the *barre* to prepare you for *this* step at the *center*.

They might also explain the details of a step, such as, when you do a tendu, 'you must brush the floor and think of going under the floor.' This is so that you fully engage all the right muscles in your leg and you will look like you have an elastic energy when you do the tendu. As a result, it will look more beautiful.

A good teacher may also give you images to help you engage the brain. Engaging the brain is a powerful tool. There are so many times I surprise myself by using the power of the mind.

For instance, my teacher tells me that when I move my arms in a port de bras, I must imagine that I'm moving my arms through water. When my arms are too stiff coming down from a 2nd position, she asks me to imagine I'm stroking a beautiful silk gown. To engage my fingers more in movement, instead of having fingers like knives, my other ballet teacher asks me to imagine wearing Spanish sleeves that have frilly ends at the wrist.

5) How you feel

This is different from how the teacher makes you feel. The only feeling you need to determine is to **feel that you are making progress**.

Teachers make us feel emotional quite often.

They may inspire us and make us love ballet more, or they might make us feel like giving up and grow to hate learning ballet! Often they make us feel both ways depending on the session.

We are not all the same. Some of us flourish under encouragement and praise. Others do better under pressure and under demanding, strict, or unreasonable teachers.

There were times when I left class feeling so discouraged, to the point where I believed that I was unsuitable to learn ballet, that learning ballet at my age was silly and frivolous, that I didn't have the right body, that I didn't have a drop of talent, that the teacher hated me, etc. I felt like I might just quit!

I couldn't believe someone could make me feel this way in my adult years.

Sometimes you think your teacher is too brutal and there's not much you can do about it. These extremely 'hard' teachers are decreasing in numbers and they usually belong to the 'old-school' generation.

They may be so frank and mean because these teachers teach the way they were taught, back in some prestigious ballet academy, where not a single hair could be out of place. Though I personally believe these strict kinds of teacher are not usually suitable for adult ballet, I know some of my adult ballet dancer friends really enjoy such strict teaching, as they would like to be taught as though they were in a pre-professional school.

This is the point that you have to remember. Good teachers are hard to come by, especially for the adult ballet dancer. Thus, we have to appreciate them even if they are a little harsh or even if we wish that they would be nicer in class.

Professionals trained in China and Russia commonly say that their teacher never once said "good work" to them or praise them openly. I'm not saying that that is the best way, but what I know is that they have been trained to be mentally tough. Throughout their careers they will continue to be criticized for their art and will get corrections as they work on each piece of a ballet company's repertoire.

I added this last bit of information to perhaps help gain a little perspective on how good dancers are produced in spite of the harsh environment they are trained in, so you do not evaluate whether a teacher is good or not by how he or she makes you feel.

Chapter 14: Private Lessons for Adults

Another way for the adult student to progress quickly and efficiently is to take private lessons.

These are one-on-one sessions with you and your teacher. You typically have to book your own dance studio and organize the session with the teacher.

In some countries, you are able to find affordable studios, which can be as low as twenty dollars, or better yet free. You can either use a school or church dance studio, and in some apartment estates, there are studios that can be booked for personal use. You may also ask your teacher for recommendations and they usually are able to help you locate a studio at a discounted rate.

Private lessons range from half an hour to about 2-3 hours, depending on you and the teacher. My first ever private lesson was half an hour, and it was spent learning how to plié.

Would I recommend private lessons?
Yes, especially for the adult.

Some ballet books and ballet teachers do not recommend private lessons and say they are detrimental to learning. There are some reasons for that, such as it is believed that the students will not be able to handle the pressure of being in a classroom.

Others simply believe that students learn better in a classroom environment. Some feel that learning under the constant watch of the teacher, such as in private lessons, may lead to developing low self-esteem, because the teacher is 100% on what you're not doing right and it is easy to get frustrated and impatient with oneself.

It may be true that private lessons for the general young ballet student are unnecessary, but it is different for the adult. First of all, the adult does not have the same luxury of time, as they do not have years and years of ballet training. They do not have the same patience to progress at the same way the young student progresses.

Let's compare the child-student and adult-student. The child who enters pre-professional training at a vocational ballet school would have spent perhaps a whole year in their first year or so, doing tendus and assembles. Adults have learned much more in the same amount of time, though not at the same precise level.

Further, it is not quite realistic to train an adult the way pre-professional students are trained. They have different bodies, goals, and expectations. You don't have to reach their level of technical proficiency to dance and enjoy ballet (though one should always aspire to).

Secondly, we adults unfortunately do not often have the luxury of that pre-professional environment and teachers who care that much.

As explained earlier about the nature of open classes and transient and busy adults, we cannot expect teachers to treat us as pre-professional students.

Thus, many adults, such as myself, get through this problem by choosing exam syllabus classes, training with pre-professional students and taking many private lessons. In fact, I attribute most of my success, breakthroughs, and improvement to private lessons.

I find that the one-on-one attention is highly effective as I save time by clarifying my understanding immediately. Instead of receiving (if you're lucky) one or two personal corrections per class, which might cost $20, I may receive up to 25 corrections. Each correction may be repeated throughout the 1.5 hour long lesson, which helps to reinforce it.

I have developed bad habits due to the nature of open classes. It is unlike professional school, where they have daily classes for 6-10 years. Children who study in those environments will find it hard to escape the eye of their teacher, who they see every day. They have no choice but to develop the correct technique under their teacher's careful watch.

For instance, for a long time I did a side port de bras (arms above the head bending sideways towards the barre) not knowing that:

1) My arm was covering my face;

2) I should bend slightly diagonally instead of sideways and flat (due to my body type and flexibility).

I was only corrected during a private lesson, or rather the teacher only noticed me then. I became mortified knowing that I had been doing it incorrectly all that time.

Another thing that I did wrong countless times was a lunge forward where I was supposed to keep the knee behind me straight. Where I first turn diagonal facing the barre, I was to use my hands to reach upwards in an open fifth and then lunge downwards with my right knee bent and my left leg behind me. I pointed my feet but I didn't know I was supposed to keep my knees straight. I had been pointing and bending my knee for almost two years in every class! This was also corrected in my private lesson.

During open classes, I see titled pelvises, incorrect positions, messy pathways to positions, but it is simply impossible for the teacher to correct everyone. That is why it is so difficult for the adult ballet dancer to progress. It is hard to progress in open classes.

Thus, that is why private lessons are an effective way to progress.

I mean, I have met some adult dancers who don't seem to need private classes and have been progressing nicely. They either

1) have danced before as a child for many years and so the understanding of the foundation of ballet is somewhat formed;

2) have some sort of dance background, perhaps in contemporary dance or something similar;

3) take daily classes under a good and demanding teacher;

4) are supremely talented.*

*There was one girl who I've seen in adult ballet class that I think is supremely talented. Her coordination level is at the genius level.

However, due to the nature of open classes, she still does not look like a classically trained dancer. Her feet are not fully pointed, her knees are not fully straight, she doesn't brush the floor, her positions are not quite correct, and she can't turn one nice pirouette. But other than that, she can mimic the moves and steps, and she moves in time with the music. I believe she's quite talented as her eye is sharp and she can coordinate her body, feet, and legs to advanced steps!

I believe that with private lessons, she will go far and look more and more like a properly trained ballet dancer. When she gets her technique right, the right muscles will develop and her body shape will change. Her flexibility will improve in a way that was meant for ballet.

The costs of private lessons discourage some people because they can seem so exorbitant and indulgent.

However, if you look across the spectrum of learning a skill one-to-one, for instance, learning the cello, piano, singing, training with a personal trainer, the cost of lessons are about the same.

Additionally, on the spectrum of tuition fees, there are some more expensive classes out there than private ballet lessons. For instance, once I signed up for a cooking class where I learned how to prepare a full Christmas meal, and that cost me $150.00.

I was given some notepaper, the recipe, and a pencil, and I literally sat there and watched the chef cook for three hours. Afterwards, we all enjoyed the food, but I felt that I would have learned more if I had a hands-on experience.

How often should I take private lessons?

I would say to take them as often as you can comfortably afford. There are some fortunate few that take private classes every day, and some who take them 2–3 times a week.

Most adults I know start with once a week, and either cut back or gradually increase. Taking private lessons once a week is quite common.

How many private lessons do I need?

Only you can decide that. Sure, some people learn faster than others but ballet is a never-ending journey.

You don't have to rush it; however, consistency is the key to progress. Taking private lessons twice a week for a month then disappearing for two months is not that useful. Taking private lessons also changes your approach in big classes. You will notice the kinds of corrections you get more, especially if another teacher reinforces it. I believe it helps 'drill' it into your head and your body.

Who are the people taking private lessons?

Believe me, they are not all rich. Most of these people have very ordinary incomes. They choose to cut back on spending on clothes, entertainment, restaurants, take out coffee, travel, etc., so they can spend money on ballet. That's what I do.

The progress I have made with ballet due to private lessons is extremely rewarding and it has made me feel that it is all worth it.

Of course, I have to emphasize that taking a private lesson with a good teacher makes all the difference. Please see the chapter on learning how to choose a good teacher.

Chapter 15: Dance with your Torso

One of the biggest challenges I see in adult ballet is learning to dance with your torso which includes the upper body.

Some ballet teachers say that it all begins with the torso.

The aim is to try and keep the torso as still as possible without it moving when you're executing the steps. You use your upper back to carry your arms and to do beautiful *epaulments*, and you use the muscles in your abdominals to control your legs. All this you can do without little jerky movements. If you do it right, from the torso, you will find that your dancing is more controlled and looks refined and magnificent.

Due to the sedentary lifestyle of many adults and years of walking on flat pavements, as we don't run across the park or do cartwheels in our free time, many of us have lost control of our torsos.

The abdominal muscles become disengaged when walking, and our brains have lost connection and consciousness with our core muscles. We tax our torsos and hips by driving for long hours or sitting at a desk.

Before all these flat smooth pavements were created, I'd bet that men and women had wonderful posture and nice flat stomachs with no back pain or neck pain. This is because walking in the forest or through fields was not as 'mindless' as walking on leveled concrete. You often had to watch out for loose rocks, branches, uneven ground, or different textures in the field. You would have been more aware and conscious of what you were stepping on, lest you fall and sprain an ankle. As a result, your core was engaged when you walked without being conscious of it.

The engagement of your core muscles means that it will continually strengthen and that, in turn, provides support for your back and your whole body.

How to know whether your core is engaged?

Try to punch yourself in the stomach. Trick yourself by saying you're going to deliver a hard punch, and as you do it, you'll find your body instinctively engages the abdominals. That is how you should dance. Yes, with your core engaged.

Another technique is to try and walk really fast or run in the sand or on raw, uneven ground, then touch your stomach or try to be conscious of your stomach and you'll realize that your core engages itself. This will help you understand how disengaged your core is during normal walking on pavement in an urban environment.

I find that this 'problem' of disengagement of the torso occurs in children as well, especially when they are toddlers and learning to walk. However, it soon goes away when they learn to engage their balance enough to walk and run.

It usually reoccurs when the child becomes more sedentary, for instance, if the child is doing more intensive study, which requires more sitting on the desk, or when he or she discovers computer games.

This occurs generally in more unfit children; but it is an extremely common problem in adult ballet dancers.

Unfortunately, it can't be helped because we live in urban environments and I'm sure a large portion of our lives involves sitting at a desk.

How to combat this problem of a weak and disengaged torso

Some ballet teachers recommend sit-ups and reverse sit-ups and other core-strengthening exercises. The only thing is that you'll probably have to do them on a daily basis in order to see results after 1–2 months.

Core exercises for beginners (0-6 months)

Sit-ups and other core exercises definitely help, especially in the beginning when you've done ballet for about half a year, assuming you attend class 2-3 times a week. Core strength will naturally develop with each class. You are actually training your core strength when you lift your legs to perform a develope or grand battements.

As you progress to more difficult exercises, you will realize that you probably could do better with more core strength. That is why professional ballet dancers continually work on their core independently from ballet class.

If you are a beginner and only take one class a week, your progress will be at a slower pace, so you might not realize the need for core strength for a while.

It is quite common to see a beginner not sweat at all after a full ballet class due to his/her (temporary) ignorance of ballet technique.

Develop consciousness of the torso

Most of the dancing in ballet starts from the torso. Another way to develop core strength is to be more conscious of your torso. One of my ballet teachers told me that all dancing originates from the torso, as that is where your center lies.

Though I do not have the strongest core, my core muscles have developed strength from years of doing daily ballet class. I feel my core muscles as my grand battements and adagio combinations become stronger and more controlled.

However, it took me a long time to develop consciousness of my torso. This is a common problem with adult ballet dancers. We dance without awareness of the torso. It is usually not held, or 'pulled up'. More often than not, your stomach sticks out and so sometimes when we turn in pirouettes, we fall backwards.

In other words, even after years of practice, I'm still developing and need more consciousness of my torso.

Some of the tricks I use to increase more brain connections to my torso are **touching/rubbing** my torso during class (not in a weird way). The more you feel your torso, the more your brain is forced to think about it.

I also use an imaginative technique I read about in Eric Franklin's books. I usually come up with my own imagery so that it works for me. As for my torso, I **imagine having a lighted ball with a heart shape in it placed in-between the top part of my ribs** (just under my breasts). I imagine the skin covering my ribs partially swallowing it and supporting it so the light in this ball with a heart shape can shine forth (the same way Care Bears shine their bellies). I then imagine that I have to hold this ball in that position with my ribs (closing in) and shine the light on every position I am facing.

On Arabesque or turns, I imagine **my ribs to be a huge container**. I imagine that I have little **heavy balls inside the container** and they must collect at the upper part of my ribs. Thus, their 'weight' pulls me forward and into balance.

My illustration may or may not resonate with you, but the thing is, you can invent your own imagery and watch how your body responds.

One other thing you can do is to film yourself. Get an app from iTunes that allows you to record your movements in slow motion. Ask your friend to record you and your consciousness of how you're doing the steps will increase. If there's the luxury of doing it again, record yourself again and you will improve very quickly.

Chapter 16: The Brain: Pure Mental Power

Learning ballet is extremely mental, especially in the beginning.

Some dancers say that it continues to be mental throughout one's dancing life.

Other dancers say that there is freedom when there is complete mastery of the foundation. At those moments, you can then work on how and what you want to express with each step or gesture. My current dance teacher reminds us and shows us from time to time how we can 'play with the steps'. That usually means we can perform the same combination of steps using correct technique with different expressions. One girl might choose to express more energy in one step and let her body linger in other moments. Another girl might be more lyrical than others and give extra detail to the expression in her eyes. Some dance outwardly, and others inwardly. This is what is usually called **your interpretation of the dance**.

If you would like to have a more visual picture of what I am describing, I recommend checking out YouTube: Queen of Dryads.

This search will lead to a list of ballet videos and you can watch each one danced differently by each dancer. Notice which one you are more drawn to, as we all have different tastes and preferences.

Similarly, each combination you learn in class can be danced and interpreted differently. Of course, you'll only be able to do this with more consciousness when you're at a higher level. At a beginner and intermediate level, your brain will usually be busier learning new steps, controlling your body, fine-tuning technique, and remembering dance combinations.

No improvising

Ballet, unlike many popular dances, does not encourage improvising. You can't make the step 'your own' *yet*. It has to be performed in an exact way, which means holding your head in a specific position for each step, your eyes following your relaxed fingers, your torso remains as still and as lifted as possible with your ribs and buttocks 'tucked in'. Your arms should be held by your back and your neck long, with knees completely straight and foot pointed.

On top of that, you have to remember the combination and control your body to perform those exact movements in time with the music. And you have to dance the movement in a controlled way.

And relax your neck and relax your face.

In the beginning, learning ballet can be extremely taxing mentally. You're trying to process what the teacher is saying, at the same time, you're visually trying to take in and make sense of what your teacher is doing as he/she is demonstrating the steps.

When I was a beginner, I would often squint as though I was zooming in to focus and figure out which leg closed in front or behind, or where my arms went, or which leg to pick up. It was tough! I could tell myself, 'okay, it is the right leg that is behind and I turn outwards,' but when done to music, I would still mess up the steps.

Then there is memorizing the combinations. Following somebody helps in the beginning, but you can't rely on that forever because your brain will be engaged in a different way that is not the most beneficial for personal progress. However, if you can't memorize the steps, just follow the more advanced dancer until you become more familiar with combinations.

Whenever a new ballet step is learned, your body is not used to the step and thus you feel clumsy and awkward. Doing the steps is uncomfortable. You'll probably have to do the step for at least a couple of times for it to feel more comfortable. Then you slowly work it to perfection.

At this point, a huge amount of brainpower is needed. Your brain is like a muscle in the sense that it gets tired when it is worked in new ways. Learning ballet requires you to use your brain in a new way, so often that you might find yourself mentally taxed after class.

If you don't press on and force your brain to engage (and not switch off) during the class, you will find yourself fumbling over the steps and performing them incorrectly. Thus, it is vital to also work through the mental tiredness until you develop more mental stamina.

I still find myself forgetting the steps, requirements, technique, or other nuances when I get tired during class. During these moments I know that I have to increase my mental stamina.

Mental stamina

It is important to have mental stamina. This means absolute focus and constant mental control. You'll need this mental control to think through every second of any combination, and all the precise and exact details, and do all this in time with the music. When not doing the steps, you have to focus on memorizing the combinations. When the teacher is talking about how to perform a step regarding artistry or technique, you have to zoom in and take in, visualize, and mark every single requirement.

This is the complete opposite of dancing at a club. At a club environment, you listen to some music, feel good, and let your body groove. There are no requirements, no incorrect positions, no directions to worry about, or eye lines or any conscious control of the movement.

The more you advance in ballet, the more increasingly mental the process of learning ballet becomes. It is takes a lot of mental power to control your body in a precise way, and that is what ballet demands of us.

This is what usually happens as your mental stamina increases:

As you progress, you might find it easier to coordinate your body, especially as you become more accustomed to the steps. You may now find that you no longer have to think so hard or work too hard. You can do the steps. It is easy to just let your mental consciousness go and just go through the motions **without thinking**.

That happens a lot in adult ballet.

Actually, you should then push your brain to engage in other things, such as the quality of **how you do the step.** That is how you become a quality dancer with artistry.

Mental power: Thinking every minute and every second

Going through the motions of the combination is not everything.

Feet take time to learn how to point, and knees take time to develop consciousness to learn to straighten. That is why in the previous chapter I wrote about increasing consciousness in every part of your body. In regular life, we hardly ever need to straighten the knees to their maximum. Thus, that part of the body 'shuts down' and your brain devotes more energy to other parts of the body, like the stomach. The moment we are hungry, the stomach sends a signal to our brains and our brains remind us to eat food.

Thus, we can think of bringing attention to other parts of the body that we seldom use. Ballet does that for us, but to speed up the process of learning, we can help our brain by being more conscious of our feet, knees, torsos, lower back, neck, and shoulders.

We have to be hardworking to continually engage the brain and not zone out, no matter how tempting that option is. It is similar to pushing through tiredness. It is very tempting to give up and just muddle through the steps. We have to think hard and clearly to point our feet and straighten our knees and keep our arms in a nice curve instead of them dropping to the 'chicken wing' position.

Even though I've been dancing at a somewhat intermediate or advanced-beginner level, I still have to **think hard about basic technique as I'm doing the combinations.**

When the combination is easy, I will consciously repeat in my brain to straighten my knees and point my feet. I will look for the sensations of my fully straightened knees and pointed feet. When I feel the sensation of straightened knees, my brain is then satisfied that it is correct. After constant reminders and looking for the right sensations, which could take weeks or months, the body forms a habit and then you don't have to 'look for those sensations' anymore.

It is very important for us as adult ballet dancers to continually go back to the basics and establish a foundational technique. It is also important for us to constantly use our mental power to look for those sensations. Why?

That is because we don't have years and years of doing really simple steps that result in gradual, natural progression. It will not be as hard for the child as it is for us to achieve that 'look' of ballet. Our bodies did not have the luxury of being slowly accustomed to the habits of basic technique.

As you progress in ballet, it <u>is important to still take easier classes that give you more time to 'think' about elements of foundational technique</u>. This actually helps you become a more advanced dancer.

Many adult ballet dancers think just because they can 'do' or get through intermediate or advanced classes that they are an intermediate or advanced dancer. The funny thing about dancing is that you often can't see yourself and many adult dancers have a different and often inaccurate image of themselves when they're dancing.

(We all do. That is why we have to really know how we look, otherwise our brain tricks us. The solution is to video record yourself dancing from time to time.)

The truth of the matter is that, apart from being able to get through more difficult and advanced combinations, **here is where the difference lies between trained dancers and untrained dancers**: basic technique and details of each movement.

As you advance, your eye will start to become sharper. You will be able to differentiate the dancers by their extremely pointed feet and straight knees, a sense of lightness and lift, precision, epaulment, control, absolutely clear positions, a neutral pelvis, and fluidity.

It doesn't matter if the dancer is a professional in other forms and has come to take advanced class. You will be able to tell whether he/she is ballet trained through **the quality of basic technique**.

Fo example, an untrained (in ballet) dancer could do three pirouettes whereas another trained dancer did only two. It does not mean that the dancer who did three turns is more advanced than the one who did two. The first dancer might have blazed through the turns with dropped elbows and with a 'down feeling'. The second dancer turned with control, with a two 'whipped around' feeling and remained high up her demi-pointe for a lingering second before coming down.

For an allegro combination with *ballone* (you can search for this on YouTube if you don't know what this step is), you can see those who are trained when they whip their legs in with their pelvis square to the corner. It is an exact and precise position. The untrained dancer will often mimic but whip their legs to the side with their pelvis in imprecise positions.

The more ballet techniques you learn, the more you'll be able to differentiate the trained from the untrained dancer.

Use easy classes to hone technique through mental strength

Thus, use the easier classes to think about your basics. Do not stop thinking about basic *pliés*, *tendus*, *battements*, etc. Get familiar with the sensations of your body when you consciously think about and perform them.

Do you *plié* properly before a turn?

Is your fourth position exact?

Are your knees straight?

Where is your head?

Are you spotting?

Are your arms held properly?

Are you pointing to the maximum?

Are your shoulders pointing backwards?

Is your chest open?

Is your neck relaxed?

Where are you looking?

Mental practice: Clear pictures and videos in the brain

When the combination is hard, we have to not let our brains go and just have a cloudy picture in your mind of what you're supposed to do. Rather, it has to be a clear picture. You must know where your feet go, what the linking and transitional steps are, where your arms go, and which positions you are facing. It's tough but doable.

To progress, spend time in bed going through the steps. For instance, if you're learning how to do a *changement*, picture yourself doing the step in slow motion. Before you lift off in the air, how much are you going to *plié*? Are your buttocks sticking out? Are you holding your core? Where are your fingers? Is your chin sticking out? As you lift off, are you pointing your feet? How do you land?

It helps to become really familiar with vocabulary so that your brain pulls up an image whenever your teacher calls out a combination.

Now, with smartphones and all their glory, we don't realize how useful they are for improving ballet technique. Some phones have a slow-motion video recording function and that helps to see your mistakes more clearly. These slow motion videos often show me how imprecise I am when executing the steps.

I have many personal examples of this wrong perception of what I'm doing. There was a time I was arguing with my teacher frequently, denying that my arms did not do a 'backwards-beyond-my-shoulders' move when I did a *jeté entrelacé*. I couldn't even see it on regular video but when I converted the video into slow motion, I saw it. How your eyes lie! And how sharp are your teachers' eyes.

If you don't have such a feature on your phone, you can download an app that has this feature. You can use it in two ways:

1) Check your technique and thus become more conscious of what you're doing.
2) Slow down videos of others with good technique so you can visualize the correct way of doing a step more precisely.

I find trying to visualize the steps extremely taxing. However, when I do it, I get surprised when I try out the difficult step the next day. My body is more comfortable with it and it is usually better.

Thus, now I try to do a slow motion video of my exam combinations whenever I do not have time to practice in the studio.

Mental power and stamina are extremely important in learning ballet and it is definitely more crucial for the adult ballet dancer.

Chapter 17: Learning Pointe as an Adult

Thinking about learning pointe someday as an adult? Here are some frequently asked questions specifically asked by adult ballet dancers, as well as my experience learning pointe as an adult. Please note that this is not meant to be technical advice. Please consult your ballet teacher/professional before using any information on this page.

Recently, my studio was closed for the holidays and so I decided to go back to the Singapore Dance Theatre to take my favorite adult open classes. There, I spotted some of my long-time adult ballet dancer friends. After a few, "Hey, how are you? I haven't seen you for a long time! Where do you dance now?" I noticed that they were going back to adult beginner classes and, to my surprise two of them were wearing pointe shoes.

I couldn't help but notice how brand new their pointe shoes looked. Obviously they hadn't done too much pointe work. I later learned that they decided to try going on pointe, hence, that's why they were taking the slower-paced classes. They then asked me a few things about pointe work since I had a little bit more experience in pointe than them.

That inspired me to write this chapter.

I'll start by addressing a few frequently asked questions:

Questions about learning pointe work as an adult ballet dancer

Am I too old to start pointe work?

No. Especially if you're an adult ballet dancer.

Although, I must say that the "Am I too old" is not the right question. 'Are you ready for pointe work?' should be the question you should ask yourself and your teacher.

You're not too old if you're 15 and above. If you're 70, you can still do pointe work, but you must go in with your eyes wide open, understanding your personal risks, but more about that later.

Will I be able to go on pointe?

Most probably yes.

The crux of the matter is "WHEN".

While there is a small minority of people that can't go on pointe no matter how much strength or technique they've gained. It could be that their ankles are way too flexible or too stiff.

When I say too stiff, this means that you can't form a straight vertical line from your shin to your toes when you're pointing your ankle. So far, I haven't met either type of student. I've met more people with stiff ankles that became sufficiently flexible enough over time to form that 'vertical line'.

When will I be able to go on pointe?

Let me just start by saying there are many theories of teaching pointe work, but what I'm able to write is the general consensus of the ballet professionals *that I'm currently in contact with*.

You will be able to go on pointe if you have sufficiently built up your strength and technique.

There are several am-I-strong-enough-for-pointe tests. One of which is to be able to execute a grand plié in the center with correct technique. The other one is to be able to do fondu on demi pointe in the center. This is for strength alone.

Most people are concerned about having enough strength before going on pointe. Personally, I think technique is most important, even more important than strength, simply because you can build up strength for pointe work by doing thousands of rises at the barre on pointe.

Mastering ballet technique is crucial before starting on pointe work.

Technique is the key to preventing injury

So what if you can 'stand on pointe'? It doesn't matter because, ultimately, you want to dance on pointe. You'll have to pirouette on pointe someday. If you are not pointing with 100% energy, or have established a good habit of straightening your knees, you're going to hurt yourself in the long run by wearing out your knees and inviting all sorts of complicated knee and back problems. Thus, technique is THE ULTIMATE IMPORTANT step to establish before going on pointe.

Yes, you can take some risks by going on pointe, but only if your technique is sufficient. Pointe work in general is less dangerous for adults than children, whose feet are still soft and malleable. However, if you're not careful, you may twist or break an ankle, suffer an elbow injury due to a fall, and if you're older, you might fracture a hip. These are surface injuries. The more dangerous ones are knee and back problems that surface after years of doing the wrong things.

Feet take time to learn to point fully. (My teacher is never satisfied by how hard I point!)

Straightening your knees to their maximum also takes time to establish.

Your metatarsals need to be flexible to 'lick the floor'.

All these things I'm still working on, though I'm already up on pointe.

Thus, having a good teacher is crucial because you need guidance and an astute eye to check for mistakes and dangers.

Should I go on pointe?

The common answers that you find on the Internet and in books are, "you must be strong enough", "you must be dancing for at least three years", or "you must be taking at least three classes a week".

For adult ballet dancers, I think the crucial questions I would like to ask are: What kind of classes are you taking? What kind of school do you dance in? Who is your teacher?

My recommendation is that you should find teachers that satisfy a few conditions: He/she must be strict and particular about technique (as explained above), and you should take claas with him/her at least three times a week. Most importantly, the teacher should be familiar with your body type, with your strengths and limitations as well. Is he/she interested in your success and safety?

If the answer is yes, you can approach your teacher about pointe lessons, or ask to wear pointe shoes in class.

This is easier to achieve in a small, intimate studio, rather than a big dance school with lots of different classes and numerous teachers. Of course, if you're able to 'follow' one teacher and become familiar with him/her, that situation is also possible.

So, that is the most important consideration — a good teacher's eyes and guidance for proper technique.

The second very important consideration is: How strong is your technique?

This is the problem for most adult ballet dancers, even those who have been dancing for 5-10 years. Most of them go to 'cold' studios, take lots of open classes and, unfortunately, very seldom are able to establish a good relationship with a teacher.

That is why it is sometimes better to risk humiliation and join a dance school that teaches syllabus work and enter their exam program. Of course, you'll be dancing with youths or teens more than half your age that are in better form than you, more flexible, and leaner. Yet, it really depends on what options you have and how much you want to dance on pointe.

In a studio where you have a good learning relationship with your teacher, he or she is more capable of helping you with your weaknesses and you will have a better chance of progressing as you work through them.

While it is more common to have this opportunity in a small studio, not all small studios are good because not all teachers in them are good, so again, it really depends on your unique situation.

Some common pointe technique blunders:

- Not straightening your knees fully

- Not pulling up

- Not pointing your feet fully (and with lots of energy to spare that 'comes out of the ends of your toes')

- Wrong ballet posture (i.e., with your bottom sticking out)

- No emphasis on strength or balance or control and just focusing on the 'moves'.

Dancing on pointe for the first time may feel so foreign that you might think, 'Why don't we all start learning ballet using pointe shoes?'

However, as you become more familiar with your pointe shoes, you'll realize that pointe work is simply an extension of all ballet technique. Yes, everything matters, from that *plié* to that *tendu* in those canvas ballet slippers.

Pointe technique reminders

Do lots of rises at the barre.

When you go up, don't jump up but slowly rise up. This builds strength.

When you come down, don't plop down. Slowly lower yourself down. Think 'up' as you lower yourself. Think of somebody pulling the hairs on the top of your head as you lower down. This builds control and increases the flexibility in the metatarsals.

Lifting your weight 'off' yourself on pointe

When you're on pointe, whether it is at the barre or in the center, lift your body weight off yourself using your core strength. Just as we stand in first or fifth position at the barre, we continue to stand very tall. You cannot just rely on ankle strength.

Some teachers call it 'pull up'. If you allow yourself to sink into your hips and sit on your legs (like the rest of the non-ballet-dancing population), you're going to add more stress on your knees and ankles.

Ensure that your ballet posture is correct

People looking at you on the side should be able to picture an invisible straight plumb line. Stand with an open chest, keep your ribs in, and your pelvis should remain in a neutral position. This is all fundamental ballet technique, whether you're on pointe or not. That is why I say technique is the most important factor!

Pointe fully...and some more!

You should be 100% pointing even though it is harder in pointe shoes! It is very easy to relax into a semi-pointing state. Thus, good technical habits should be established first, otherwise it is very difficult to progress in pointe work later on.

A note about ballet teachers teaching pointe

Ballet dancers, teachers, and other professionals argue a lot in ballet; they argue about what is right, what is beautiful, what is wrong, what is ugly, what should go first, how should this step should be executed, where the foot should be placed, and so on.

Similarly, there are so many different theories about who should learn pointe, when pointe should be learned, what is dangerous and what is not...

Some teachers are overly concerned about safety, while some seem to not care at all.

Unfortunately, not all teachers know how to teach pointe correctly. And how will you know if your teacher is teaching pointe correctly? You can probably gauge by the kind of corrections you get from him/her.

In fact, I think the teacher who is teaching pointe has a bigger responsibility because, as a teacher, they obviously know more than the student. The way the teacher teaches pointe is vital to a student's progress and safety.

There are many teachers who seem to do crazy things while teaching pointe, but some really know what they're doing and they know their students' feet well. Some like to separate the students into groups to do different exercises, for instance those with strong ankles will be separate from those with weaker ankles, and this also depends on the natural flexibility of their ankles.

Those who teach just because their students insist on going on pointe must learn how to pace and control the class. She could start off with 5 minutes on pointe and move on to 20 minutes, and so on and so forth. In those 5–20 minutes, most activity would be doing endless rises to build up strength.

Of course, there are teachers who just don't care. They just let anybody in the class, OR there are students who simply insist on going on pointe. I've taken classes in New York City where students who have never done ballet before pay for a pointe class and arrive with pointe shoes in hand, with no ribbons sewn. They insisted on taking the class and the poor teacher had to get some elastic and ask them to do releves with two hands holding on to the barre. She had to move on to teach class because there were other students waiting for her to get started.

Thus, the teaching method, a teacher's watchful eye, and an emphasis on the correct technique are the most important things to look out for when it comes to selecting a pointe ballet teacher.

While teaching adults pointe work has a fair share of responsibility, ultimately, you as the adult have to take responsibility and decide for yourself if it is right for you. You have to understand the full risks of learning to go on pointe.

Risks of learning pointe as an adult

My personal take: I think as adults the risks of learning pointe are the following:

- Slipping (because of the lack of control and familiarity, especially if technique is very weak)
- Not knowing how to choose the right shoe/fit for pointe
- bunions

- Fractured/sprained ankles (from falling and from lack of strength)

- Knee & back problems due to poor/wrong technique

- Fractured hips (from those who are older and are susceptible to fall)

- Muscle injuries due to overstrain/pulling

- Excessive tension in the muscles due to compensating for weakness.

Of course, there are those who will have differing views from me.

My experience learning pointe work as an adult

I started pointe when I was in my teens, therefore to come back to it again wasn't so foreign for me. However, I have had some experience with a few different teachers who had different views.

One wanted to put me on pointe after being back to ballet within four months, another would not let me try at all because of my insufficient abilities to make my 'knees more-than-straight' and to point with 100% energy. Another teacher asked me if I'd been learning pointe for more than six months before letting me attend her half-hour pointe class. One teacher I know didn't care if people just wore pointe shoes in class.

My final teacher separated the class into three sections: One group with two hands on the barre, the second group with one hand at the barre, and the rest of us in the center. This was done after the barre warm-up in pointe shoes.

Personally, I've found that learning to control your torso area and feet are two of the hardest things to master. You have to develop a sort of sensitivity to your feet and metatarsals especially.

You actually rely a lot on a strong core, and you have to activate your entire body to lift you 'off your feet' rather than relying solely on ankle strength.

My pointe struggles as an adult ballet dancer

My struggles? I tend to plop down on pointe rather than going through demi-pointe. I need to be more engaged and exert the right amount of push, lift and hold for control. Also, I need to plié more on the way down when on pointe, rather than letting my heels touch the floor first then plié.

Whatever you struggle with in ballet slippers, whatever incorrect technique or weak technique you may have, it is magnified on pointe.

For instance, I can manage my pirouettes just fine (not perfect) but I have a tendency to lean back too much because in actual truth, I struggle to keep my pelvis neutral (due the tightness of my lower back and weaker core) throughout ALL my center work. Therefore, when turning on pointe, I have the tendency to fall backwards.

I can manage a double or triple pirouette sometimes in ballet slippers, but can barely do one nice clean pirouette on pointe. I can also tell you that my get-by-spotting does not work on pointe.

I have relative ease when doing pique turns on demi-pointes or ballet slippers, and thus I am confident doing them on pointe as well.

As for strength, that is coming along nicely because we always start pointe work with lots of releves and tendus. I also take 3-4 classes a week, and that really helps with building up strength gradually.

As for pointe shoe fitting, I was fortunate to get pointe shoe specialists to fit me. While travelling to New York I visited Grishko and Gaynor Minden and booked a pointe-shoe fitting appointment. My first pointe shoes were bought in Bloch, in Australia.

I know not everyone gets this opportunity but I would advise against buying them online, especially if they are your first pair. I know some shops overcharge but if they have someone who knows how to fit you, it is worth going to them. With that being said, not everyone who works in a retail shop can fit well! It is always best to ask your dance teacher for a good recommendation.

The other struggle I had when learning pointe as an adult ballet dancer is really just finding an adult pointe class. They are so rare because of all the requirements for pointe: commitment to dancing and a good teacher, most of all. Of course, in most countries the majority of people learning ballet are not adults, but hopefully that will change.

Chapter 18: Ballet Examinations for Adults

Considering ballet exams as an adult?

Are you thinking of taking ballet exams as an adult? Here is an article about the current situation of adult ballet dancers who are considering taking ballet exams as an adult. This chapter will refer to the Royal Academy of Dance (RAD) examinations that adults can now take.

While I'm not the best person to ask about RAD examinations in general, I can share with you my experience specifically if you're an adult ballet dancer who is interested in doing RAD examinations someday.

In the past, up until about 2000, adults could only take Grade 6 ballet exams in the graded syllabus. For the rest of the levels, including the vocational ones, there was an age limit.

Beginning in 2000, there is no longer an upper age limit for ballet examinations. (Hurray!) *Please note that this is what my ballet teacher said to me at that time in Australia. I'm not sure if it is the same situation throughout the world.*

However, in spite of this change, adults from around the world are having difficulty finding a teacher or studio that will accept them. That is the general feeling I get from adult ballet dancers who have emailed me. However, I can speak from experience, especially in regard to my own country of Singapore.

Why is it so difficult for an adult to take ballet exams?

Though there is no longer an age limit to take RAD examinations, it is still hard for adults in general because there is no real basic RAD class that caters to adults. The graded syllabus from 1-4 is generally catered to the way children learn, which is highly different from adults.

Most ballet studios/schools or ballet teachers generally discourage adults from taking ballet exams, or in this case RAD ballet examinations. Why? They reason that ballet exams are only for dancers who want to turn professional, or who want to consider teaching ballet as a career.

Since most adult ballet dancers are pretty much content with their profession and aren't likely to have a shot at turning professional, most ballet studios turn them away.

There are legitimate reasons for this:

Adult beginners may be disruptive to the class. Most of the teenagers or children in RAD classes have been dancing for at least 4-6 years.

Adults may not be able to cope with syllabus classes. Since most adults dance in open classes, they might be shocked that the teacher will not stop the class to teach them the more complex center work of the syllabus.

Adults may find these syllabus classes boring and repetitive.

Ballet teachers require high commitment (attendance) to these classes in order to prepare them for exams. An adult's schedule may not allow for this.

Schools and RAD registered teachers risk their reputation if their students fail RAD exams (results of students' performance on examinations are recorded). Hence, they are reluctant to send in adult beginners.

Some schools simply prefer to keep their classes within certain age limits. These schools are probably stuck in the old days, before 2000, when it was nearly impossible for adults to participate in the RAD syllabus.

Why do adults still want to take ballet exams?

One of my friends who teaches adult ballet did a poll on her website asking how many of her adult ballet students would still like to take ballet exams, despite not wanting to pursue a ballet career of any sort.

And the results were that more than 50% said YES!

I can understand some of the reasons why adult ballet dancers still want to take RAD exams, because they are more or less similar to my own reasoning.

Firstly, they want to feel a sense of achievement.

Ballet is a long hard road, sometimes with no end in sight. A certificate saying that you've passed your examinations helps to quantify your efforts. You'll have something to show for all the money and time that you've invested in learning ballet.

It is easier to measure your progress in learning ballet if you are preparing for an exam.

A progression of levels that the RAD syllabus offers provides a roadmap or benchmarks in your learning.

It is hard to measure personal progress. Some teachers don't even tell you how much you've improved. Even if they did, you wouldn't have much of an idea. Some of my friends measure progress by how many pirouettes they can do. That is not the only way! Allegro (jumps and beats) are more solid benchmarks, in my opinion.

With exams, you'll have a clearer idea of your progress.

The ability to learn variations (dance numbers)

I remember wanting to join a syllabus class just so I could learn the examination variations, which consist of one classical dance number and another contemporary ballet variation. I also wanted to learn the port-de-bras and adage combinations.

In adult open classes, we might get a two-minute dance variation if we're lucky. It changes every week. We don't get to learn and perform to a full song, which is rewarding, even if it is just for your video camera.

That's part of the fun...though admittedly, you'll probably get really sick of your examination dances and center combinations.

Exams provide a systematic way of learning.

The way most adults learn ballet around the world is in open classes. This means that there is no set work and the teacher is free to set whatever exercises he/she wants, regardless of whether or not you've actually learned the steps properly.

For instance, I never quite learned Balancé (waltz) properly until I had to learn it while taking an advanced syllabus class. I mainly imitated my dance teacher in adult open classes. My foot wasn't licking the floor like it should and my arms looked really curt.

Choosing to learn ballet through a syllabus means that you'll get time to learn each step properly.

Repetition & artistry

Some of my adult ballet friends scoff at examination ballet classes. They try for a couple months or so and deem it as 'extremely boring'.

Why? This is because in RAD classes (this is for some schools, not all) the same examination music is played while we dance the set examination barre and center exercises. It is the same old thing week-in and week-out.

I used to get bored, too. But after a while, I enjoyed the freedom my mind had to think about other things, such as how I was performing the step, without trying very hard to memorize the combinations (and not mess them up).

This way, you actually get the chance to perfect a step and SOLIDIFY it in your muscle memory and your brain.

I've since realized that there are so many ways to do the same step correctly, but adding your own interpretation is what makes you a different dancer compared to someone else who is technically as good. This is what is known as artistry.

In open classes, you seldom get a chance to work on this, unless of course you've been dancing for 5-10 years.

I really appreciate the learning connections in my brain since I've started syllabus work. I've learned to see how many other combinations are just like the ones in my RAD syllabus class, only a little different. That way, it takes up less brain power to learn other combinations in my open classes.

Another way of learning

Taking ballet exams, even if you don't have to, can be viewed simply as another way of learning. The pressure you put on yourself will enable you to push through your own personal limitations. All of us can relate to how exams force you to memorize, and quickly, because of an upcoming assessment.

Would I recommend that adult beginners take ballet exams?

It depends on what you want out of learning ballet.

But if you ask me, my answer is generally no, unless learning professional ballet is an unfulfilled dream.

You can't decide to take ballet exams casually because it will require a lot from you, especially with the limitations of being an adult ballet dancer (mostly lack of time for the muscles to develop muscle memory).

If you really enjoy the culture of ballet (i.e., taking class, dressing up, using ballet as a form of activity or workout, learning steps, being comfortable in a beginner's class, watching ballet performances, etc.) then you really don't need to take ballet exams.

Ballet exams require a high commitment in time, energy, and finances. The stress of it all might put you off ballet! I know it did for some of my friends.

If you have been dancing ballet for a long time and you are interested in perhaps teaching other adults or children, then yes, get started on the Intermediate level RAD examinations (minimum requirement to apply for their teaching certificate).

If you are open to exploring different methods of learning ballet, then perhaps you could commit to a syllabus class for a year (which is what it takes to really learn the syllabus with an examination perspective) and decide at the very end if you want to enter for exams (or let the teacher decide).

I'm not saying that I'm better than my friends who didn't take ballet exams, but I felt that my progress could be felt more clearly since undergoing examinations because of stricter training.

Are you taking RAD exams as an adult? I would love to do an email interview with you! Drop me an email at seira@balletlove.co.

Your story will inspire other adult ballet dancers. You can share how the process works in your country and how many people at different adult ages are doing RAD ballet exams. It seems more acceptable at dance studios overseas than here in Singapore.

If you're a dance school offering the RAD syllabus to adults, please email me! I want to create a worldwide directory of major cities and countries that offer adult ballet dancers the chance to take examinations.

Chapter 19: Why I Choose to Take
Ballet Exams as an Adult

I took the RAD Intermediate Exams as an adult.

This section will cover how I did my RAD (Royal Academy of Dance) Intermediate exams as an adult, as well as why I did this, and my training and exam experience.

Lots of people ask me why I would, in my adulthood, take RAD Intermediate exams. It didn't make sense to them. I wasn't going to be a dancer, or teacher, or pursue any sort of career in the dance world, so why take RAD exams?

Why I chose to study the RAD syllabus as an adult

For one, I took RAD classes when I was little, and later when I was a teenager, so I had fond memories of them.

Secondly, I had been going to adult ballet classes/open classes for a while and felt the lack of precise training.

Thirdly, I wanted to dance...I remembered learning variations and port de bras combinations and I enjoyed them. I wanted to dance a variation instead of the 20-second variation at the end of an adult ballet class.

Fourthly, I noticed the difference between the adult ballet dancers who had been previously syllabus trained (when they were a child/teen) and those who started learning ballet in open classes (it doesn't matter if they had prior dance training or not). There was more artistry in those who were syllabus trained and I wanted that.

Later on, I would add this reason: It gave me a chance to work on my foundation of ballet training. The basic principles of classical ballet are everything!

Adults in a RAD syllabus class

Depending on where you live, getting into an RAD class might be a challenge. However, it is getting to be more widely accepted and more widely available. (See the RAD ballet exam levels.)

Traditionally, there was an age limit in each class. By the time you were 15 or older and didn't have continual ballet training, you were usually thrown into Grade 6. That was the reason why many of us, even those who learned ballet as a child, couldn't go back to our old ballet schools. We didn't have anywhere to go. Thankfully, the Royal Academy of Dance changed its system and now there are no age limits for ballet examinations.

Unfortunately, most ballet schools and studios took a long time to adjust. There are still snobby schools that ask you how old you are, and will not let you take classes with their school even though you passed at a certain level or have taken RAD examinations, just because you're an adult. It doesn't matter that you've swallowed your pride and are willing to take a class with 14 year olds!

Your best bet is to email RAD in your country directly, or its headquarters, the Royal Academy of Dance in the UK, to ask for schools/studios teaching its syllabus. You can either call or email those schools and ask if they allow adult ballet students in their classes. Be prepared that you might have to do an audition.

That's what I did. The studio I first contacted was snobby to begin with and refused to let me into the Intermediate class (even though that's the level I stopped at) because I had no certificate to prove it. I started with Grade 6, very soon after got asked to join the Intermediate Foundation, then Intermediate, and then got asked to join Advanced in the span of a year. (I progressed quickly because of extra private coaching.) However, I found a more suitable studio and switched, and did my RAD Intermediate exams with them.

In the RAD Intermediate program at the new studio, there were about 10 adult ballet students ranging from 21–45, with only two in their 20s alongside a class filled with girls ages 12–16. As the year progressed, eight of the adult ballet students dropped out, and only I and the 21-year-old (who technically just turned 21) progressed and complete the examinations.

Frankly, it is a huge commitment to do RAD exams, whether or not you're a young teenager or an adult. Most of my adult ballet dancer friends didn't quite understand that.

You have to take class almost everyday, do intensive stretching on your own and maintain your body. You can't really go off on holidays or skip class to have dinner with friends. It is mentally tiring too and can be stressful because there are very specific objectives to achieve.

It also doesn't mean that if you get through the combination means you are doing it correctly. It is also a very long (probably year long) tedious process.

My training for RAD exams and experience of exams

The following is a journal entry I wrote for my Ballet Diaries, April 2, 2013:

I took my RAD Intermediate exams yesterday. I started training for the exams a year and half ago, though I had to spend an extra 6 months prior to that to get back in shape from not dancing consistently for the last decade. Getting back into shape was pretty intense. I lost 5-6 kg (12 pounds) in the process, became flexible, and my posture has been better ever since.

Of course, I had nvested a lot into it, seeking the best teachers I could find, reading, taking lots of good classes and visiting my physiotherapist to loosen those stiff muscles I gained from working at the computer for years.

It wasn't the RAD organization or the syllabus that I particularly cared about, but it was the specific training for exams that I was after. It was a system of learning and I felt that it worked for me.

I put in slightly more than a year of training for this particular exam. It was boring. It was the same old barre and same old music time after time. The center work was indeed challenging for me. It took me so long to finally remember the steps. I had to become so familiar with the steps before I could work on the quality of the movements.

I remember that it took about 8–10 months before I really felt comfortable doing Allegro 2 exercises. It was only in the last three months that I felt I could cope with it and not become filled with fear and dread each time it was our turn to do the exercise either solo or in pairs. Up to the last month, I still made the occasional mistake of doing a glissade derriere instead of a glissade devant.

I had many breakthroughs, which strangely occurred in the last three months prior to the exam. In fact, 80% of my breakthroughs occurred in the last month. I think it had something to do with the fact that I was doing the entire syllabus over and over again, which caused something to happen to my muscles, plus there was the powerful effect of watching myself on video.

In the last two weeks before the exam, I had myself recorded doing the entire syllabus five times. I would record myself doing, say, the Adage exercise, then watch it, see what I didn't like, become more conscious of what I was doing, and then record again, repeatedly.

Of course, this was dependent on how long the patience of the person who was recording me would last before running out. Yet, watching yourself and then applying the corrections is amazing for improvement. I believe you can save yourself months of classes, depending on your teacher, who may only correct you sporadically. That is why private lessons are important for those who need to catch up.

(Note to self: Buy a proper video recorder with its own stand so I can stop pestering my friends to record me.)

When the exam time came, I was nervous for sure. But I enjoyed being able to dance with a live pianist. I messed up a bit on the free enchainment, but carried on with the exercise. I smiled (though not the full-on cheesy smile) and performed as best as I could.

Everything went relatively well with little or no mistakes, though of course my pirouettes could have been cleaner. Reflecting back on the experience, I was so consumed with performing that I wonder if I pulled up enough, if my ribs were in, my knees were straight, and if I pointed my toes as best as I could. I'll never know...I just hope my muscle memory kicked in enough.

Now that the exams are over, I feel a huge sense of accomplishment. I think back on the breakthroughs I had during the process and they are numerous:

Breakthroughs

1) Linking steps are smoother

2) Developed the artistic side of dancing the step; being 'gentler'

3) Having a more elegant carriage of the arms

4) Being able to dance with my chest pulled up and ribs in

5) Being absolutely comfortable with pique turns on both sides

6) Doing doubles en dehor and en dedan (though they could always be cleaner and more reliable)

7) Understanding what it means to pull in opposite directions, pulling up as you go down

8) Mastering Allegro 2 and Allegro 3

9) Learning how to do a little lift of the arms and legs before going down

10) Learning how to hold the arms form the back, not from the shoulders

Ballet training that still needs work
(These are things I need to work on):
1) Keeping the knees straighter all the time

2) Grand jetes

3) Keeping my core and back engaged all the time

4) Ribs in all the time

5) Pointe with 100% energy, right now I'm pointing with 60% and thinking it's 95%

6) Establishing classical poses and becoming more familiar with the 'travel paths' of arms and limbs

Doing the Intermediate exams also meant a couple of things for me. I had always wanted to take the exams back when I was 18, but I was too afraid of the 'free enchainment' component to enter. I'm glad I achieved my childhood dream. Passing the exam meant that I now had access to the more advanced classes and more specific training — the kind you don't get in adult ballet classes or open classes.

It also means because I will have obtained a certification of completion, and I will no longer have to go back to the kiddy classes. I can proudly say I have a 'right' to be there. Of course, it means nothing really in the real sense of learning ballet, but at least I have a choice in terms of what class to take. Before, without any certification, in my experience at least, the teachers will always put you in the classes with the young girls. Being an adult who fiercely believes in good training, I had to suffer the humiliation of taking class with these young girls for many years.

At least in the advanced classes, though there will most certainly be some younger girls present, there is a wider age range of women, and there will be those who took their ballet exams then went overseas to study, or got married, had a baby, and came back to do class. I feel more comfortable in these types of classes.

So, that was my objective, maybe some people might find it silly, but at the moment, it works for me.

Chapter 20: How to Take RAD Exams as an Adult

This is my story of how I managed to learn the RAD ballet syllabus as an adult and eventually take RAD exams.

This section is based on a diary entry I wrote about how I managed to take the RAD exams in Singapore. It might be easier to take RAD exams as an adult in other countries. I can only speak for the country where I studied ballet. Write to me if you are taking RAD exams as an adult: seira@balletlove.co.

As I wrote in earlier chapters, I had done a bit of ballet as a child and learned the RAD syllabus, but I had no examination certificate to prove it. A few of my other adult ballet dancer friends managed to 'pick up where they left off' and take RAD ballet exams because they had a certificate to prove it, even if it had been 10 years prior.

Adults in general face lots of difficulties if they want to learn the RAD syllabus and eventually take ballet exams. Ballet studios and teachers have good reasons for being hesitant, of course. Adult beginners have lots to work on and can be disruptive to the class. They have to cope with learning techniques and the lengthy syllabus work.

So how did I get around these road blocks? This is my story:

No RAD adult ballet class in Singapore

After dancing in adult open classes for a while, I started to notice the difference in adult dancers who were trained in the RAD (Royal Academy of Dance) syllabus when they were younger. I felt they had better technique and artistry. Thus, I resolved to look for a RAD class.

I called a few ballet studios/schools in Singapore and all of them said that their RAD classes were for children only.

I emailed the Royal Academy of Dance Singapore and asked for schools. The woman I spoke with gave me a list of schools that had RAD-registered teachers.

RAD registered teachers are considered better than non-registered in general (though not necessarily) because RAD registered teachers have to pass RAD Intermediate exams from the vocational syllabus at the minimum, and undergo a rather detailed training program, which is approximately two years of study.

This is of utmost importance: Find a good teacher

There are many not-so-good teachers in Singapore who are teaching ballet. Many of them have poor ballet technique and you or your child will probably not benefit from their classes.

I once met the boss of chain of ballet stores in Singapore when I was buying a pair of pointe toe pads. He asked me where I was dancing. I said, "You know, open classes at SDT but I'm training for my RAD Intermediate exams independently."

He was probably feeling generous and chatty that day, as he went into his office and pulled out a really old RAD information guide and proceeded to tell me there was room for more RAD registered teachers in Singapore. He seemed passionate in raising the ballet standards in Singapore.

He was annoyed that many teachers aren't qualified and are bad teachers, yet they populate the ballet schools in Singapore. We chatted a bit about ballet. He then tried to convince me to go for my teaching certificate once I'm done with exams. He even ended our conversation with an enthusiastic, "I hope you become a RAD teacher!" as I left the shop.

First of all, I was very flattered to be mistaken for a serious ballet student, even though I was past 30. I've come a long way since before my body was more shaped like a ballet dancer as it is now. In the beginning, ballet shop assistants used to eye me suspiciously and assume that I was shopping for my child. When I told them that I was shopping for my leotard, they either didn't have sizes or seemed pretty snobby about it. Nowadays, they just look and me and say, "Looking for pointe shoes?"

Secondly, if only they knew how hard I had tried to get a teacher who was willing to teach me and enter me for exams!

The following describes how I did it.

Be prepared to take class with people half your age.

After I called up the list of schools that RAD Singapore gave me, I pretty much received the same response from every studio: They don't take adults.

However, a few invited me down for an audition. I was worried that my technique would be insufficient, thus, I decided to watch some classes as though I was a parent, of course as discretely as possible.

Since I am an adult beginner at ballet, my technique wasn't sufficient. Thus, I wanted to speed up the process and started to engage in private classes. After all, that is how some of my adult ballet dancer friends did it (and Natalie Portman, too.)

Prepare for your audition: Learn the syllabus

I started with a good private teacher. Of course, I had to try different private classes with several ballet teachers before I found the one that I felt was the best. He helped me establish a good foundation before helping me learn the RAD syllabus. After private lessons for a few months, I then had the courage to audition for a few ballet schools.

(At that time, I did not know that my current teacher could have introduced me to his dance contacts, so I didn't ask him to.)

An audition for a class in Singapore simply means you take a trial class with the current students. The teacher will then see how you hold up and if your technique is sufficient to keep up with the class.

Some schools wouldn't even consider adults, even if they were open to audition. So, I tried this tactic further, saying that I would not be entering for exams. At that time, I only wanted to develop the technique and artistry of syllabus-based learning and had no confidence in myself to take ballet exams.

But saying this worked. Hearing that I wasn't planning on taking exams, some big-name schools allowed me to do the trial class and possibly join as a student there. Of course, I then had to face the humiliation of dancing with teenagers more than half my age...

Work hard and take private classes

During my private classes, I learned the syllabus and that helped my audition process. I could do the exercises along with the girls in my class and was even leading them in the examination dance. That way I convinced the teacher that I was serious and I knew my work.

All three schools I auditioned for accepted me after my trial classes. I even started dancing at all three schools to figure out which environment was best for me and eventually selected the class I would prepare for exams in.

However, preparing for the exams took me over one year. I was also completely committed. I took lots of class, read books, worked on my own, stretch endlessly, watched the examination video over and over. I maintained my body, ate well, slept well, didn't travel and say no to all those events that clashed with ballet class. It would also have taken a longer time if I hadn't supplemented with private classes.

There are many others who didn't need that extra coaching. The teachers wouldn't let me take exams because there was no way my technique would have improved enough. Private classes were the only way to keep up with the class! Then again, that's me; you, on the other hand, might be a brilliant and talented dancer. I've seen some of them in my class!

Also, I've recognized that learning the RAD syllabus and taking exams is merely a means to get better at ballet technique. It is NOT THE ONLY WAY. Taking examinations does not prove that you're a better dancer; nor does it means that you're a serious ballet student. So, before you work really hard to find a teacher who would enter you for exams, ask yourself first if you can make a commitment for gruelling ballet training and also make sure that the teacher is a really good one (thus worth it), and not just trying to take your money.

Chapter 21: Tips and Techniques
For the Adult Dancer

Progress comes in different ways.

More often than not, you'll find yourself progressing exponentially in the beginning as you become more familiar with ballet. After a while, you might feel as though you've hit a plateau.

In this chapter, I will share some ideas and ways for you to keep progressing and overcome those moments of plateauing.

Adult dancers often progress quickly with learning coordination, ballet terms, and getting through the class. However, it is common that all these adult dancers will soon feel limited and feel as though it is hard to progress or they can't seem to do more advanced steps no matter how hard they try.

Even if they do manage some advanced steps, they will not be performed cleanly and they often feel unbalanced and insecure, which will make the dancer feel far from confident.

Why?

There is only so much you can achieve by mimicking ballet movements in open adult ballet classes. Adult ballet classes are different than the classes for children because they do not have the luxury of time. The steps that are covered in one adult class will often take years for the children to master. Unfortunately, most adult classes focus on coordination, and very little on technique.

Good coordination helps with learning technique. Both must be worked on consistently.

Real ballet technique is where the secrets of classical ballet exist.

It is the reason why some adult dancers progress and some don't. Some may dance in adult open classes for 10 years and are even in advanced classes but not progress in the sense that they cannot perform movements cleanly in the correct classical way.

Here are some ideas to keep progressing:

- **Formulate a general vision/goal of what you want to do.**

Keep a ballet diary or journal and write down your goals for the week. It is better to have small but detailed ballet goals. That way, each goal is more achievable. Repeat them before class and review. Add a tick if you felt that you have done it. Your goal could be to practice one pirouette or allegro step at least three times after class or stretch and hold for five minutes.

- **Choose a teacher to follow**

Build a good relationship with your teacher, that way your teacher will be familiar with your strengths and weaknesses and will consistently remind you of your mistakes.

- **Choose a class and commit to it**

Progress can only be made when there is commitment.

- **Keep healthy**

Eat fresh, healthy foods, sleep well, and hydrate, hydrate, hydrate. I also take supplements and extra protein like an athlete.

- **Roll out/press out your tight muscles**

Go for deep tissue massages as often as you can, especially when you're dancing at a higher level. Tight muscles are more prone to injury. Buy a foam roller and press out those tight muscles. Now that we're dancing as adults, we can't quite afford to lose momentum to heal, nor do we want to cope with pain when we're dancing. Thus, it is our responsibility to look after our body very carefully.

- **Stretch**

If possible, make this a habit. Your dancing will become better and easier if your stretch regularly.

- **Strengthen your core**

We need core strength for health, whether we dance or not. Do sit-ups as part of your warm up routine!

- **Watch and attend the ballet**

Go to live performances, borrow ballet DVDs from the library, or watch performances on YouTube. There are many lovely ballet videos that will certainly inspire you.

- **Visualize**

Train your mind to dance in your head. As you're doing a step, zoom in on important details in your mind's eye; where is the leg closing? Are your feet pointed?

- **Read ballet books, especially those about technique**

This will give you a different perspective and help you approach your learning of ballet better.

- **Record yourself dancing on video**

It is amazing what you can learn from watching videos of yourself. How you think you dance is often not the same as reality. This will help you self-correct and give you more accurate knowledge of your dancing.

Then, go over the videos in slow motion and write corrections for yourself. You may also ask a friend who is better than you for feedback.

- **Spot**

Practice spotting. As adults, our necks are stiffer and slower to whip around. It is important to maintain neck flexibility by doing neck rotations or massage and practice, practice, practice. This is especially true if you want to advance to the higher levels of ballet.

- **Practice releves and balance**

The more you practice this, the better your turns will be. Stay up as long as you can.

- **Make ballet friends!**

Whether it is another beginner, professional, or a teacher, you can always learn from somebody. If a beginner asks you for help, by explaining the step, you will also become aware of how much you know or don't know. Beginners also bring a different perspective to learning ballet.

Being friends with pre-professionals or professionals is beneficial because you can ask questions or they might give you tips on how to improve. These are valuable sources of information.

The mirror lies

Our eye for ballet and technique takes some time to develop. If you're a beginner, your eyes cannot really 'see' yet.

This means that what we see in the mirror isn't exactly always the truth. Our eyes only perceive something. They take in selected information from the mirror and our brains recompose the image.

Personal perception is quite a funny thing. This explains why many people who can't quite sing well think they are good enough to go into an audition for the X-factor. Their brain perceives them to be better than they are. They sound better to themselves than they do in reality.

That is also why I used to look at certain dancers and wonder if they're professional. After a while, I became more accurate. Now I secretly laugh to myself when beginners ask me if I'm professional! It's still flattering to be mistaken, but I know why they think this; it is because their eyes have not developed yet!

Often when we look in the mirror while dancing a step, we might think we are doing it perfectly. We might even feel beautiful or think we're graceful. Many times, we can't see our mistakes and they are glaringly obvious to a teacher.

This is also why we must choose to study under teachers whose eyes do not miss anything.

Developing a sharp eye to see what is correct or beautiful takes years. As you take more classes, your eye for perfection and beauty will increase, so you will grow more accurate in determining what is correct in ballet.

But for now, don't trust the mirror. Sad to say, for a long time, it is usually not as nice as it looks. Trust the video sometimes, but mostly trust what your teacher tells you.

Relying too much on the mirror will also make you a slow learner. Always dance while seeing the movements in your mind's eye. Try it and you'll see how much faster your body reacts!

Learning/linking steps

When you first start out in ballet class, you'll find yourself learning each exercise by itself. You'll start with plies, then tendus, glisses, jetes, rond de jambes, fondus, grand battements, and so forth.

When you have finished at the barre, you will then proceed to do a few exercises in the center. These exercises are comprised of stringing individual exercises at the barre. You then have to think ahead of yourself and try to make the transition from one step to the other smoothly.

There is also a variety of *linking* steps that you will probably learn in the center. These are connecting steps that help you make your life easier by moving from one step to the other. A lot of them are travelling steps. This means that these steps will help you move across the room by dancing them.

They may be hard, but learn them well so that they get into your muscle memory and you won't even have to think about them.

When I started, I was very honest with the teacher. I requested for him to slow down in his demonstrations. I don't know if the other more advanced adult ballet dancers were annoyed with me but I couldn't figure out what he was doing.

Thankfully, he would demonstrate the step and let the more advanced group mark the steps, and then he would slowly demonstrate the exercise to a small group of us, the ballet newbies. I got to learn properly how to do the glissade, both with change of foot and without.

Another problem I had is that I was too jerky during the execution of the combination. I wasn't used to thinking ahead. I would do one step then fully stop whatever I was doing and try to figure out the next step. This resulted in a loss of fluidity and grace in dancing.

Most beginners will go through this phase. How do you overcome this jerkiness and improve fluidity? The best way is to mark the steps or do the steps over and over and over until, as dancers put it, the steps "get into the body."

My personal breakthrough about linking the steps together only came after I trained for my RAD intermediate exams. I had a set of fixed exercises to memorize and dance to, which I did for a year. It 'got' into my body such that even after a year of NOT doing the exercises, such as a variation (dance number), I could still do them when I heard the same music. In fact, I did that just today!

Because the steps became so ingrained in me, when I attended open classes (with no fixed steps or syllabus), I was able to link steps better because I began to see the new steps as variations of my exam steps. In my mind, I would think, 'Oh, that's quite similar to my exam steps, just that this arm goes here, and my leg changes front instead of back.' My brain had established new connections and it made more sense to me than how I previously tried to dance.

Of course, taking ballet exams is not the only way to learn linking steps. It also comes with practice and taking more classes. A few adult ballet dancer friends I know would go over steps they felt difficult during class, AFTER class. I think that is a great method as well.

The general pattern I see for learning to link steps is to not give up. Just find someone to stand behind, follow them, and try to do the steps on your own after class. The more you practice, the more your body gets used to the steps and the more information you can absorb, like technical details, because the same parts of your body become 'auto-pilot'.

Once you learn to link steps, it's going to be on a whole new level where you learn how to go through every microsecond of the step, instead of from count to count, or worse, position to position. Dance is flowing movement. **It is not about getting from one position to one position** (personal reminder to myself). The way to do it is to increase consciousness and control over every step. There has to be a purpose in every motion. You have to first dance with an 'engaged' mind until it gets into the body, then you let your emotions flow. That is the more technical aspect of ballet dancing.

Elasticity & fluidity

The concept of dancing with elasticity and fluidity is linked to musicality. I watch some teachers yell at rather advanced dancers about 'dancing in time with the music'. The reason why they are not in time with the music is because they are dancing without fluidity or elasticity. They dance as though they are chopping garlic on the chopping block. They dance like a broken doll, jerky and jittery.

For a long long time my dancing was jerky and jittery. I didn't know I wasn't fluid due to the open classes I was taking. Teachers would correct technical errors in those classes and there was not much time left for artistry. You can dance correctly, but not look pretty.

For example, it was tendu front.

Stop.

Tendu back to first.

Stop.

Tendu side.

Stop.

I was merely moving my legs to specific positions.

This is akin to getting up from a chair in chopped up movements, which may go something like this: You first place your feet on the ground. *Pause*. Then straighten your knees. *Pause*. Then shift your weight onto your feet. *Pause*. Then straighten your back.

TADAH!

I don't think anyone moves that way. We get up from our chair in one fluid movement.

That is why my teacher says we have to stop thinking of our exercises as chopped up movements. For instance, if we had to dance a combination of '*3 tendus to the front, one to the side, and 3 to the back*', it is not a total of 7 movements. It is ONE movement.

Also, as beginners, when we haven't developed our stamina yet, we tend to take mini breaks; we place our foot to the front and relax for a while until the next musical note then we move it back to the position. So we're actually not dancing *full out*, or using our full energy and fully engaging our muscles.

This may also explain why certain dancers have more toned legs than others.

Bouncing ball

Our dancing should be elastic, like a bouncing ball. If you look at a slow motion video of a bouncing ball (check out YouTube!), it accelerates then slows down and repeats. So our tendus, plies, fondus, and our dancing in general should reflect this quality. It should be smooth, controlled and we should be able to see energy in the movement, or a certain force. It shouldn't look lifeless or loose.

Drawing imaginary lines

Another way of thinking about this is to imagine every movement you make will be drawing lines on paper, except that you're drawing lines in a 3D space. Whenever you completely stop, instead of 'slowing down and then accelerating like a bouncing ball', you break the line. The objective and challenge is to keep drawing the line and thus make the longest line but not break up the movements into little steps; make it one fluid movement.

Energy lines like light beams

I like to imagine that I have light beams that come out of my fingers, feet, and head. The more energy I send out, the longer light beams extend beyond my body. So as long as I'm sending out long light beams, my energy is sent out beyond my fingers. As a result, I'm engaging my muscles and they will not look indifferent or weak. I will move with a purpose. This helps my movements become elastic and not broken up.

Performance

If you have a chance to perform, do it! It will increase your dancing knowledge by leaps and bounds. The way you will approach class will be different too, you will be more focused and be more conscious of the details.

Learning to dance with others is also another important dance experience, as you not only have to consider what you're doing alone but with others as well. The goal is to dance as one.

Costumes are also fun, and dancing in them is also another experience that you won't get in class. With performance, you'll learn the art of stage make-up, the ins-and-outs of what it takes to put on a show. And you'll get to experience what it is like to dance with nerves. Usually, we're at 70% of our best! We also learn how to cover mistakes and cover others' mistakes.

If you don't get a performance opportunity, organize a small show for yourself or for friends and family, even if it is in front of a video camera. Put on the best performance for the video camera! You can organize what you're going to wear, what you're going to dance, hair and make-up and all that. It would be something that you can keep, watch, and remember for the rest of your life.

As you are preparing for the performance, your teacher will help you edit and fine-tune all the details until you look as lovely as possible when you're dancing. One then realizes how much detail goes into dancing ballet.

Last Words: Where to Go from Here?

Ballet is a long long journey. The good thing about this journey for us is that it is mostly a pleasant one. We don't have to worry about auditions or competitions or getting kicked out of a professional program. We can dance at our own pace and determine how much effort to put in and how far we want to go.

Mostly, we have to keep healthy and fit and make a commitment to dance.

Many of us have dreams of being able to do a double pirouette, fouettes, or dance on pointe. Sometimes we say, "If I can get up to her standard, then I'll be satisfied and happy." Then we find that we're not satisfied with doubles, now we want to do triples...

I thought you should know now that this goes on for a long long time. So try not to think of absolutes but enjoy the process of your progress.

It is also natural for us to compare, just to gain some benchmark of how well we're progressing as dancers.

The hard reality is that, even for us adult ballet dancers, there will always be someone with better technique than us. They might also be more talented, or have better feet or a body that is more suitable for ballet. It is not exactly a good use of mental energy to compare ourselves. Instead, try to focus on how to make your dancing more beautiful.

The more I dance ballet, the more I realize that it is about the journey. We should **savor every bit of it because the day may come when we can no longer dance like we're dancing now**. We might move to a place where there isn't a ballet studio, a new baby may come, our suddenly due to circumstances we can no longer afford ballet. Many things can happen that may prevent us from dancing.

That is why I try not to take my ballet life for granted. Although I complain of aches and pains or frustrations, I want to remember how awesome and blessed I am to be able to dance; to be able to wear a leotard, tie my hair back, and dance to some of the most beautiful music on earth.

I pray and hope that all of us will make a commitment to dance no matter what, for as long as we can.

Thank you so much for reading this book. I hope this book has given you some ideas on how to progress and improve. Most of all, I hope that you will continue to enjoy dancing ballet and enjoy the journey as an adult ballet dancer!

Made in United States
Orlando, FL
04 December 2024

55002665R00114